Mount Mer...
1711-2011

Aerial view in 1960's, looking towards Deerpark and Mount Anville. (Aerofilms)

Joe Curtis

First Edition: 2011

Published by:
First Return Press,
23 Upper Mount Street,
Dublin 2, Ireland

© Copyright: Joe Curtis, 2011

ISBN: 978-0-9533320-6-9

All rights reserved. No part of this publication may be used, displayed, copied, scanned, photographed, stored in a computer, shared, or transmitted, without the prior written permission of the copyright owner.

Cover: Aerial photo by Peter Barrow

Contents

Acknowledgements

Many thanks to all the following for permission to use maps and photographs, or assistance. After each photo or map caption, the source is abbreviated in brackets in a smaller font.

National Archives of Ireland, and the Director of the National Archives of Ireland: NA1

National Library: NL

Irish Architectural Archive: IAA

Valuation Office: VO

Trinity College Map Library: TC

Gilbert Library and Dublin City Archives: GL

Dun Laoire Rathdown County Council: DLR

Sacred Heart Nuns: SHN

Little Sisters of the Poor: LSP

Dominican Nuns: DN

Christian Brothers: CBS

UCD

Seamus Kearns (postcards): SK

Kevin Harrington (photos in IAA): KH

Scoil San Treasa: SST

Peter Barrow Photography: PB

Morrisseys Auctioneers: MA

Finnegan Menton: FiMe

Simmons Aerofilms, England: Aerofilms

The Fitzwilliam Museum, Cambridge: FM

ESB

Biotrin

Most other photos by the author, although a few are from unknown sources.

4

Chapter 1

FITZWILLIAMS

This family came to Ireland at the beginning of the 13th century, initially living in Ballymun in north Dublin. By the beginning of the 15th century, different family members were living in Donnybrook, Thorncastle, Merrion, and Booterstown, the latter having previously been the property of John Cruise and John de Bathe. In due course, the Fitzwilliams acquired large tracks of land in south Dublin and further afield, much of it granted by the King/Queen at a very low rent. At the height of their powers, their Dublin estate stretched from Ringsend to Blackrock, and inland to Dundrum and Ticknock. However, the Roebuck estate of Lord Trimleston cut into the Fitzwilliam estate at Old Merrion, stretching up to Mount Anville. Various branches of the Fitzwilliam family had castles at Dundrum, Baggotrath, Thorncastle (near Ringsend), and Old Merrion (between Ringsend and Blackrock). By the early 18th Century, they abandoned Merrion Castle, and built a new residence in the civil parish of Taney, naming the demesne Mount Merrion. The old castle ruins were removed in 1780, and another house called Merrion Castle was later built about 50 metres south of the old castle. In 1865, the new house, and about 30 acres of land, was bought by the Sisters of Charity, who moved their "St Marys Asylum for Female Blind" here from Portobello House in Rathmines. The nuns built a chapel on the site of the original old castle, and demolished the newer house.

Merrion Castle by Gabriel Beranger, about 1766. (NL)

The **Civil Survey** of 1654 describes the parish of "Tanee", and contains the following useful information (using the same spellings):

"Colonell Oliver fitz Williams of Meriyoung, Irish Papist, had land at Dondrom and Ballintry, by estimate 6 ploughlands, or 500 acres, comprising 20 acres of meadow, 300 acres of arable, and 180 acres of mountain and bog. The proprietor acted as Major General in the Irish Army. There is on the premises, one castle, slated, and a barne, one garden plot, and a small orchard. The premises were a Mannor, and kept Court Leet and Court Baron. The tythes belong to the College of Dublin".

"Matthew Lord Baron of Trimleston, Irish Papist, had land at Roebuck, by estimate 4 ploughlands, or 400 acres, comprising 12 acres of meadow, 360 acres of arable, and 28 acres of pasture. The proprietor acted in the Irish Army as Coll' of horse, and passed the said lands as his inheritance in Anno 1641. One castle, which was destroyed by the Rebels, and one garden plot, one mill in use worth in Anno 1640 tenn poundes. The tithes belong to the College of Dublin".

"Lord fitz William of Meriyoung, Irish Papist, had land at Owenstown, by estimate 1 ploughland, comprising 4 acres of meadow, 60 acres of arable, and 4 acres of pasture. The proprietor did mortgage the premises in Anno 1638 to one Lieutenant Robert Cooke who hath possession thereof. The tithes belong to ye College of Dublin".

"Maurice Archbold of Kilmacud, deceased, a Papist, had 1½ ploughlands, comprising 15 acres of meadow, 60 acres of arable, and 20 acres of pasture".

When **William Petty** surveyed (**Down Survey**) the "Parrish of Doonabrooke and Tanne" in 1657, it contained the following townlands (amongst others):

Dundrum and Ballinteer	Oliver Fitzwilliam (Irish Papist)	562 acres.
Roebuck	Baron Trimleston (Irish Papist)	500 acres.
Owenstown	Lord Merrion (Irish Papist)	100 acres.
Kilmacud	Morris Archbold (Irish Papist)	150 acres.
Ballally	James Walsh (Irish Papist)	440 acres.

Petty reported that the quality of the soil in the parish of Tanne was arable meadow and pasture, and stated "there stands in Dundrum a castle in repair; in Roebuck another; and in Ballally another". In the townland of Merryyoung was a fine stone castle and a grove of trees. In the adjoining "parrishes of Kill and Mouncktowne", we find the following townlands (amongst others):

| Booterstown | Lady Reeves (Protestant) | 285 acres. |
| Stillorgan | William Wolverston (Irish Papist) | 370 acres. |

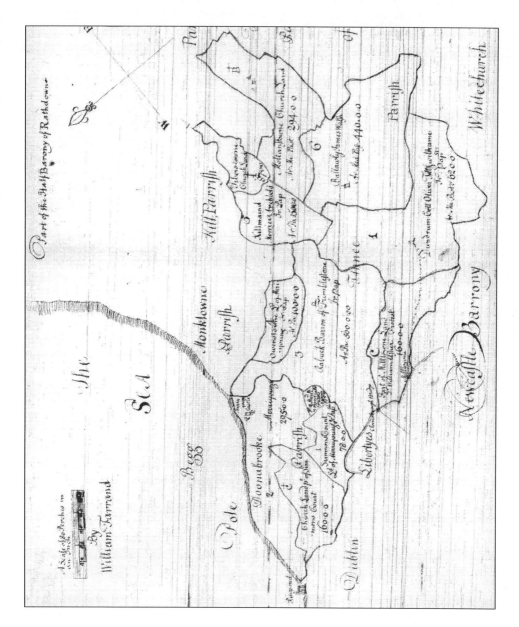

Down Survey, 1657: Tannee Parish.   Owenstown is in the centre - 100 acres. (NL)

7

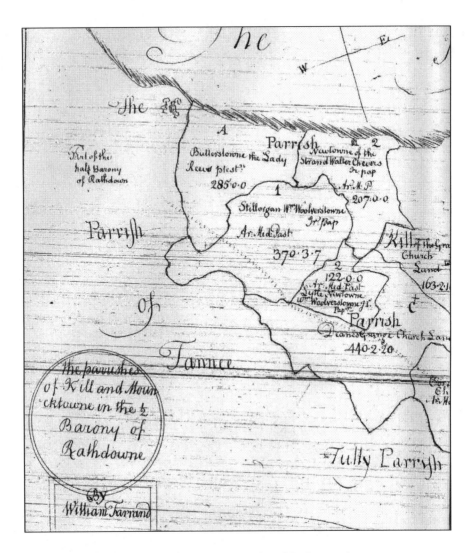

Down Survey, 1657. **This map interlocks with the previous page.** (NL)

The **Census** of Ireland, circa 1659, shows how sparsely populated this part of the countryside was, and lists some important people, although not necessarily the landlords:

Dundrum	Isaac Dobson	14 English, 33 Irish
Rabucke & Owenstown	William Manly	5 English, 25 Irish
Rabucke		2 English, 17 Irish
Stillorgan	Henry Jones	13 English, 25 Irish
Kilmacud		11 English, 2 Irish
Booterstown		41 Irish

In 1629, Sir Thomas Fitzwilliam, of Meryon, was created the first Viscount Fitzwilliam. Oliver was the second Viscount, William the third, Thomas the fourth, Richard the fifth, Richard the sixth, Richard the seventh, and John the eight, upon whose death in 1833 the viscountcy became extinct. However, most of the family property had been willed in 1816 by the seventh Viscount to his cousin George Augustus, Earl of Pembroke and Montgomery, and thereafter the estate was known as the Pembroke Estate. Historians recall that in 1169, Richard de Clare, Earl of Pembroke, but otherwise known as Strongbow, arrived in Ireland at the request of Diarmuid, King of Leinster, married Diarmuid's daughter, Aoife, as a reward, and then, King Henry II started the conquest of Ireland. Some of the Fitzwilliams are buried in Donnybrook Church graveyard, beside the present Garda station.

There was no such townland as Mount Merrion, and the townland of Owenstown (100 acres) corresponds only partly with the present layout. In later years, Mount Merrion was also known as Callary. "Papists" was the term used for Catholics, ruled by the Pope in Rome.

The Fitzwilliam family are thought to have built their new home in Mount Merrion around 1711, because a date-stone was found on the stables in recent decades, and has now been fixed to the present Community Centre. By this stage, Richard, 5th Viscount Fitzwilliam, had converted from Catholic to Protestant, in order to take his seat in the Irish House of Lords - "he conformed to the Established Church", to use the phraseology of the day.

Much can be learned about Mount Merrion from examining the Pembroke Estate papers, held in the National Archives. A map of the estate, dated 1722, by Cullen, shows a large two storey, five bay house directly opposite the main east avenue, flanked by two smaller three bay houses. However, when Dublin land surveyor, Jonathan Barker, surveyed the property in 1762, his map shows all the original buildings demolished and replaced by a different arrangement, with the main house on the north side of the avenue, and extensive stables and farmyard on the south side, but nothing facing down the east avenue towards the sea at Blackrock. The new house was built as a north and south wing, connected by a long passage, with kitchen and servants quarters in the north wing. Therefore, the datestone/keystone of 1711 is not original to the stables, and was probably on the original house facing down East Avenue.

Barker calculated 84 acres in the demesne, and listed various buildings and fields as follows: new kitchen, kitchen yard, new stables, hackney stables, hen yard, working shade for stone cutters, cow house, cow yard, horse pond, dung yard, ash grove including vistos (south of stables), pleasure garden with terrace walks, elm wilderness (west of stables), lawn at back of house, scotch fir grove, with octagen shell house in centre supported on stone pillars and 32 vistos corresponding with the points of a mariners compass (now Deer Park Wood), furry park, Owenstown meadow, wood field, well meadow, rushy field, shelly field, St Patricks field (north-east of demesne), quicken park, shoulder of mutton meadow, pigeon park, lower slang, upper slang (both previously called long meadow, and now site of Trees Road), and quarry field.

Barker's 1762 valuation also listed the townland of Owenstown, around the present-day Fosters Avenue. Plot 1 was retained by the landlord. Plot 2/3 was being used illegally by the Honourable John Butler (also known as Major Butler), who had built himself Butler's Lodge. Plot 4, including a house and garden, was leased by Butler, although he had sublet to a merchant. Butler also leased adjoining land from Lord Trimleston, alongside Mount Anville, and seemed to be trying to tie the two lots of land together. He was a troublesome tenant for the Fitzwilliams, and was accused of spying on them over the boundary wall! Plot 5, including a house, was let to George Spring for £5, 9s (this was later the site of Owenstown House). Plot 6, comprising 24 acres, was let to Anthony Foster, for a comparitively low rent of £11, 16s. Plot 7 was let to George Quin for £24, 2s, 6d., and Plot 8 to William Langford.

Barker also provided information regarding the size of the Pemproke Estate in 1762, as follows:

Baggot Rath	276 houses	620 acres
Old Merrion/Simmonscourt	12	272
Booterstown	60	310
Mount Merrion	1	84
Owenstown	7	89
Dundrum	12	1,096
Great Bray	20	226
Total	**388 houses**	**2,700acres**

The acreage was equated to 4,373 English acres, and produced income of £2,233 per annum.

Within a few years of Barker's map, an extension had been added to the front of the house (the south side of the south wing), but the design was in poor contrast to the original house. When the estate agent, Elizabeth Fagan, wrote to Lord Fitzwilliam in England 1767, she referred to a letting to Lord Bristol, and that the tenant intended installing chimney pieces and grates (fireplaces) in the new part of the house. The agent then tells Lord Bristol's secretary not to waste any money on refurbishing the house, as Lord Fitzwilliam intended demolishing it in the next year, but this plan was never acted upon.

The 18th century demesne initially extended only to the present Roebuck Avenue, and not to Foster's Avenue, and did not include a Deer Park to the west of the woods. The 6th Viscount Fitzwilliam is credited with forming this Deer Park in the years preceding his death in 1776.

By the time William Ashford sketched the layout of the demesne around 1805, the property extended as far as Fosters Avenue, and westward to Mount Anville estate. By 1831, a new Deer Park had been added (the area around the present Cedarmount Road, which was known as Callery, and originally the property of Viscount Allen). Ashford depicts the residence as being two distinct buildings, the main one (showing the new south extension, with most of the original house obscured by trees), and a separate north wing, which was the servants quarters, all described as The Lodge. This implies that the estate was being used as a hunting lodge, and hence the house was quite small compared to the seats of other important land owners. In fact, the Fitzwilliams rarely lived in the house, since their main residence was in Salisbury, England, and they usually rented out the house from year to year, although maintained control over the surrounding land. The extensive stables, a short distance to the south of the main house, pointed to hunting activities, and the farmyard adjoining the stables shows that the estate was used partially for farming purposes (hen yard, cow yard, dung yard, horse pond), etc.

The stable block (a large part of which is still in use as offices, at 93, The Rise), is shown on an 1831 map as having residential accommodation near the south end of the main building, and likewise there is a small residence attached to one of the glasshouses in the extensive gardens. The north wing of the stables facing the main house was nearly as imposing as the house, and may have been used as steward's quarters at a later date, although a chief steward's house was erected in the gardens in the 1890's, and is now in use as a private house (No 29, Trees Road). Over the years, the two wings of the main house were substantially united, as extensions were built between them.

The Fitzwilliams seldom occupied Mount Merrion House, except for short periods or special occasions, since their main and more palatial residence was in England. One exception was, Richard, Sixth Viscount Fitzwilliam, who died in the house in 1776, after carrying out various improvements to the estate. Instead, the Fitzwilliams let the house to important people, such as the Honourable John Wainwright, Baron (Judge) of the Exchequer in the 1730's,

11

then to the Lord Chancellor, Robert Jocelyn, in the next two decades. The accounts show that the Chancellor paid annual rent of £34,10s, and that he vacated in 1756. John La Touche occupied for a few years in the early 1780's, at a rent of £162/pa. Another notable in Mount Merrion House from 1786 to 1793 was the Attorney General, the Right Honourable, John Fitzgibbon, better known as Lord Clare. Thereafter, the 1800 Act of Union decreased the importance of Dublin, and shifted all power to London. Richard's will of 1815 in fact left Mount Merrion House and demesne to the use of his agent, Richard Verschoyle of Merrion Square, and Barbara, his wife, for their lives, and their survivors.

The Fitzwilliams, and later the Pembrokes, were absentee landlords, and employed Estate Agents (Agents) to run their affairs. These agents sometimes occupied Mount Merrion House, especially during the first half of the 19th century, but in later years, the estate office was alongside No. 1 Wilton Place, near Baggot Street Bridge, in the heart of the main income-producing properties (the Pembroke Township). The most well known agents were Bryan Fagan, and then his wife, Elizabeth, in the middle of the 18th century, then their daughter, Barbara (later married to Richard Verschoyle, who died in 1827 in Mount Merrion House), following by Cornelius Sullivan, John Vernon, and finally his son, Fane Vernon. Fane was a barrister and Justice of the Peace, and his involvement ended around 1923. Around 1970, the office moved from Wilton Place to 14 Fitzwilliam Place. No 1, Wilton Place is now an ESB crèche, and the adjoining estate office (built in the late 1860's) was demolished to make way for an office block, until recently occupied by NIB Bank, and now a new office block known as 7/8 Wilton Terrace. The accounts for 1766 show that Elizabeth Fagan was paid a salary of £100 for collecting the rents of the estate, while her assistant, John Cantwell, received £40, which was a lot of money in those times. All the workmen in Mount Merrion <u>shared</u> an average weekly wage bill of £1, 10s.

1 Wilton Place, 1970's. (IAA).   Pembroke & Montgomery logo
on 1 Deerpark Road.

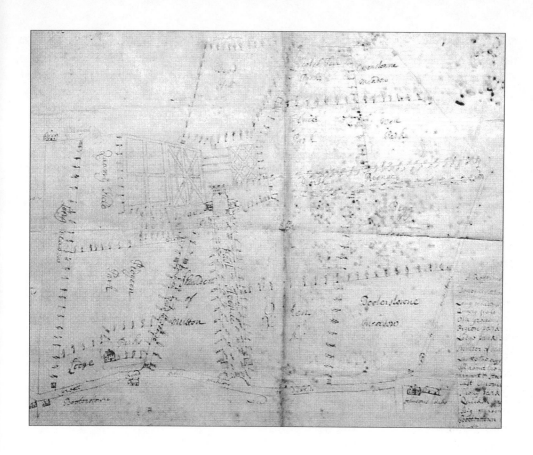

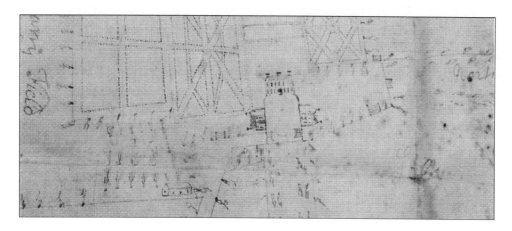

Cullens Map of 1722, showing main house facing the driveway (east avenue), flanked by two smaller houses. (NA1, Pembroke Estate, 2011/2/1/7)

A **Government Act of 1842** (Private) was enacted to allow the family to manage their estate better, partly by permitting the grant of leases to third parties in Ireland, and partly by selling off ground rents in England. The First Schedule of that Act lists their rented properties in Dublin, and some details might be of interest, to illustrate how wealthy the Pembrokes were.

They rented a total of 372 large houses in Georgian Dublin, comprising 57 in Merrion Square, 9 in Merrion Street Upper, 73 in Baggot Street, 37 in Lower Mount Street, 19 in Upper Mount Street, 6 in Wentworth Place, 6 in Grattan Street, 18 in Moira Place, 10 in Warrington Place, 6 in James Street East, 30 in Fitzwilliam Street Lower, 28 in Fitzwilliam Street Upper, 16 in Fitzwilliam Square, 31 in Leeson Street, 9 in Lower Pembroke Street, and 17 in Upper Pembroke Street. There was also a Coach Factory in St Stephens Place, rented to William Whitsill. Only a few of the houses were vacant, awaiting new tenants.

In Baggotrath, they rented 20 acres and a large Distillery to Robert Hay. Several small dwellings at Balls Bridge were let to two different tenants, who presumably sub-let them. Three dwelling houses and gardens on the Circular Road were let to one man. Five dwellings and gardens in Sandy Mount were let to one man, in addition to several small dwellings to another man, and several small dwellings, gardens and land to a woman.

In "Old Merrion", a dwelling house and 9 acres were let to Dominick O'Reilly. Miss Nowlan rented "Slated Dwellings, Nursery and Pasture Land" of around 60 acres. Richard Thwaites rented "Several small Houses, Gardens, and Land in Whites Avenue" amounting to over 16 acres. Mary Fegan rented a "House, Garden, Pleasure Ground, and Land", totalling over 37 acres. James Connolly rented "Several Dwelling Houses, Gardens, and Land", totalling over 42 acres.

Seven tenants rented houses and land in Simmons Court, totalling over 80 acres.

In Booterstown, about 246 acres were let to 18 tenants, and most plots contained "several houses and gardens and land". Colonel Henry White rented over 25 acres, including a House (presumably St Helens), Garden, Pleasure Ground, and Land. Other tenants were James Ormsby, William Oglevie, Dr. Wilkinson, Arthur Ormsby, Rev. John Pomeroy, John Verschoyle, Catherine Fegun, John Roe, John Gillineve, Robert Barry, Isaac Dolien, William Vavasour, William Metcalf, James Fitzmaurice, Thomas Kelly, Isaac Dolin, and Richard Jones.

In Owenstown, 49 acres were let to Colonel Hall, comprising House, Offices (toilets), Gardens, Pleasure Grounds, and Land, comprising Merville House. J. Turbett rented a little over 12 acres, of similar description, comprising Owenstown House.

In Dundrum, David Sherlock leased over 9 acres, including a house, offices, gardens, and land.

In Bray, about 250 acres were rented to 18 tenants, and they in turn sub-let a substantial number of small cottages, and a few houses.

At the bottom of the scale ("property ladder" in modern parlance), about 45 two-storey houses, and a similar number of cottages, in Irishtown (now part of "Dublin 4") were let to 26 tenants, occupying no more than a few acres. Thomas Murphy was the most interesting tenant, because his holding is described as "Baths, Garden, and Yard", extending to 0 acres, 1 rood, and 9 perches".

On the following two pages are the annual accounts of the entire Pembroke Estate in Ireland for the year 1859/1860, with receipts on one page, and payments on the opposite page. Note the salary of £1,200 to the estate agent, Mr Vernon, including his Clerk, Mr Norman. In 1853, the amount was £1,000. When Cornelius O'Sullivan was the agent, he did not receive an annual salary, but instead received a percentage commission based on the amount of rent he collected, thereby giving him an incentive to reduce arrears of rent, which could be very substantial in some years. As an example, his commission in 1847/1848 was £1,058, based on rent received of £21,174, even though the annual rental was approx £24,000. In passing, Major Fairfield was the agent in 1851, before the appointment of Vernon.

Moving forward to 1914/1916, the rent roll was around £36,000, and the agent Vernon was in receipt of a salary of £1,700, making him a very prosperous man, since this was equivalent to more than ten times the average industrial wage for that era.

Substance of *Mr. J. E. Vernon's* Account of the Estates *of The R...*
in the *City & County* of *Dublin &c* for *One* Years' Rents due *at Mich...*

RECEIPTS.

Places	Annual Rent			Arrear on last Account			Total due at the above date			Allowance			Received			Arrear on this Account				Total received		
City Rental	7790	19	.	111	9	9	7902	8	9	15	.	.	7814	16	5	72	12	4	G. Austin for old Materials	100	.	.
																			John Brady for Do.	20	.	.
Reversionary Do.	5847	1	10	159	16	2	6006	18	.	.	.	.	5916	3	8	90	14	4	C. Lindsay for building a Wall and levelling ground at Simmons Court	30	.	.
																			One years dividends on Sandymount Church Fund	57	19	6
County Do. Including Rent charge	13377	19	1	359	13	7	13737	14	8	29	15	.	13060	18	4	647	1	4	Dublin & Kingstown Railway Co. one years dividends to Oct 1859	35	3	10
Temporary Lettings	37	3	7	4	16	.	111	19	7				41	6	7	.	13	.	One years Interest on Mount Jerome Cemetery Shares to March 1859	13	15	.
	27053	3	6	635	17	6	27689	1	.	44	15	.	26833	5	.	811	1	.	Amount received from Children at Ringsend School	11	3	8
																			Sundry arrears of Rent received	25	10	.
																			Amount received from the Court of Chancery in the Matter of the Estates of Visc. Fitzwilliam	1008	14	3
																			James McFadden for Reconveying of Charge on the Donnellan Estate	825	.	.
																			Total Rents Received	26833	5	.
																			Total Receipts £	28954	11	3
																			Add Balance on last a/c	9749	9	6
																				38704	.	9
																			Deduct Payments	28227	2	8
																			Balance at the Provincial Bank of Ireland (carried to Next Account) £	10476	18	1

Bray Trust Estate

Lady day 1860

	Annual Rent			Arrear on last			Total due						Received			Arrear				Total received		
Total Rental	717	3	10	4	5	4	721	9	2	.	.	.	695	19	11	26	9	3	Total Rents Received	695	19	11
																			Add balance of last a/c	548	15	6
																				1244	15	5
																			Deduct Payments	866	11	7
																			Balance in Bank £	378	3	10

Pembroke Estate Accounts for 1859/1860: Receipts of £28,954. (NAI)

PAYMENTS.

FOR ESTATES.	£	s.	d.	FOR ESTABLISHMENT.	£	s.	d.	Miscellaneous £	s.	d.	Agency and Remittances £	s.	d.	Total Payments £	s.	d.
Rent charges &c	580	12	4	Mrs Lacey, Servant at Mount Merrion	24											
Income Tax	974	4	0													
Assessed Taxes & Tithes	835	3	2	Mrs Nist, Housekeeper Do	21											
Fire Insurance	28	6	9	Do Board Wages	24											
Subscriptions & Donations	830	19	-	D. Welsh, Gardener Do	55											
Buildings & Repairs	551	7	4	Incidental Expenses	13	3	4									
Roads retaining walls, fences and improvements	1013	3	1	Sundry Bills for Mr & Mrs Herbert	151	4	9									
Houses, Gardens, Plantations and Draining	1351	10	5		288	8	1							288	8	1
Pensions & Annuities	68			Mrs McJennett Bray for purchase of Ground for new Road				150								
Schools	135	2	3													
Allowances to Tenants	20	11	11	Mrs Thomas for surrender of House Burlington Road				150								
Caretakers Salaries	70	15	6													
Office Messenger Salary	26	10	-	Last instalment of expenses in opposing the Kingstown Waterworks Bill				70								
A. Ramsay, Steward at Bray	59	17	-													
W. Carter Clerk of Works	200	-	-	Repaid J. Neill for money paid by him to Butler in advance for Grazing 1860				60								
Do for Mapping Leases	28	-	-													
Brassington & Gale for Valuation	78	11	6					430						430		
Incidental Expenses	72	5	11													
Law Costs	276	6	7													
	7201	7	6											7201	7	6
				Mr J. E. Vernon 1 years Salary including Mr Norman as Clerk				1200								
N.B. Salary raised from £1000 to £1200.				Commission on Newport Rental							50	6	2			
				Stationery & Stamps							57	11		1307	7	1
				Remittances to Messrs Hoare & Co							18600					
				Cash to Mr Nelting							400			19000		
											Total Payments £			28227	2	8

Bray Trust Estate

	£	s.	d.
Rates Taxes and Income Tax	37	14	5
One years head Rent to 29th Sept 1859	136	3	2
Provincial Bank for Interest on broken sums to 24th Sept	159	13	-
Do Do to credit of a/c No 2 on account of Loan of £7500	500	-	-
J. E. Vernon Commission on 695.19.11	33	1	-
Total Payments	866	11	7

Pembroke Estate Accounts for 1859/1860: Payments of £28,227. (NA1)

17

Pembroke Estate Accounts for 1914/1915/1916. (NA1)

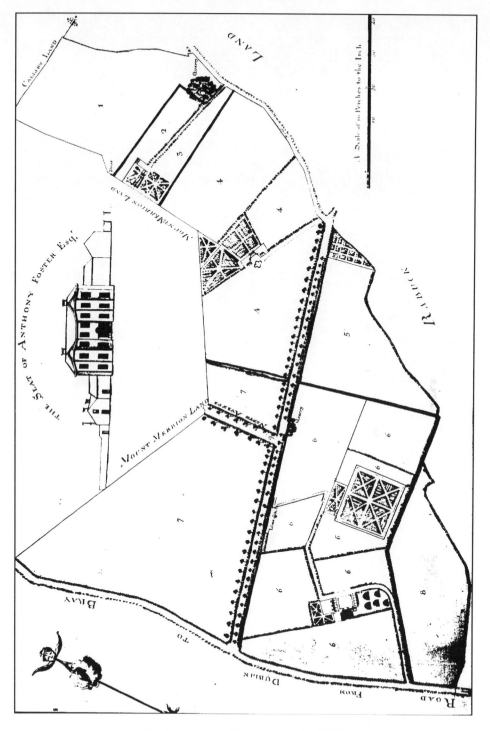

Barkers map of Owenstown in 1762
(present N11 along bottom, Fosters Avenue up through centre).
Merville on right, occupied by Anthony Foster. (NAI, Pembroke Estate, 2011/2/2/1)

19

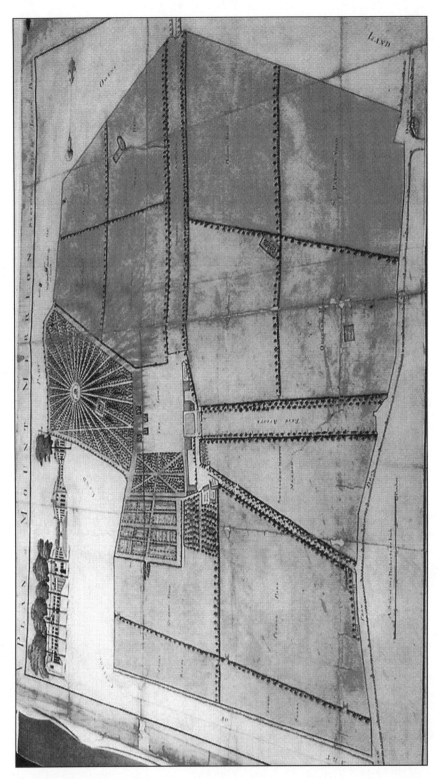

Barker's map of Mount Merrion Demesne, 1762. (NA1, Pembroke Estate, 2011/2/2/11)

20

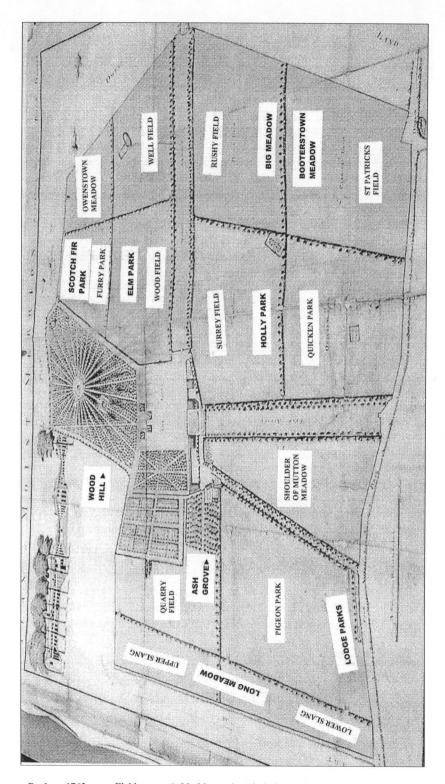

Barkers 1762 map. Field names (added by author) in bold are from Cullens map of 1722

21

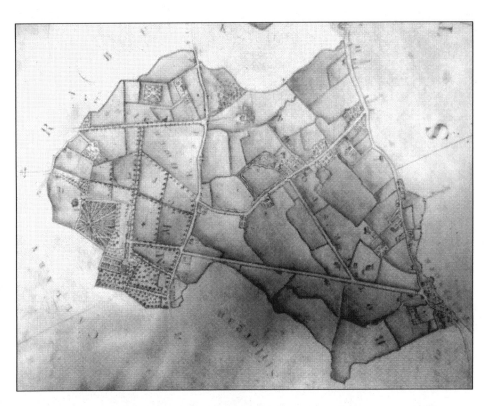

Roe's 1774 map, with Mount Merrion on left and Booterstown on right. (NA1, Pembroke Estate)

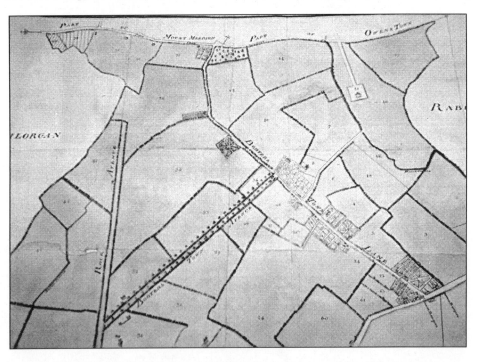

Barker's 1762 map of Booterstown: Mount Merrion Avenue is not completed. (NA1)

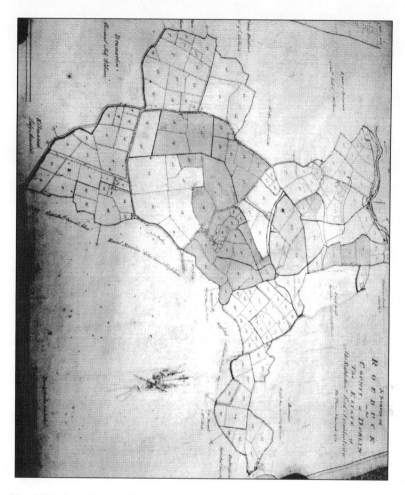

Part of Lord Trimleston's estate shown on 1783 map of Roebuck (slots in to left side of map below). (NA1, Pembroke Estate)

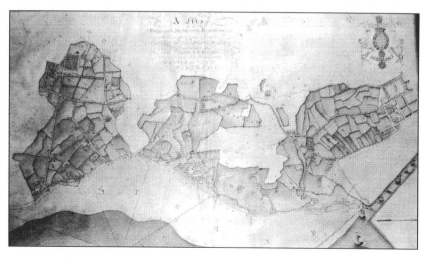

1774 map: Mount Merrion/Booterstown on left, Stephens Green on right. (NA1)

Colour painting by William Ashford, 1805.
Looking east, stables on extreme right, Lodge in centre (substantially hidden), and servants wing on left. (FM)

Sketch by Hamilton Verschoyle, around 1824/27. Probably more accurate than the earlier painting, which used "artistic licence" to show a view towards Howth. (NL)

Sketch by George Augustus Montgomery in 1826 (from east drive). (NA1)

Ashford colour painting, 1805: Stables. The building on the right is now the site of the Scouts and Guides Hall. (FM)

Ashford colour painting, 1805: House, from East Drive. (FM)

Ashford colour painting, 1805: House, from south. (FM)

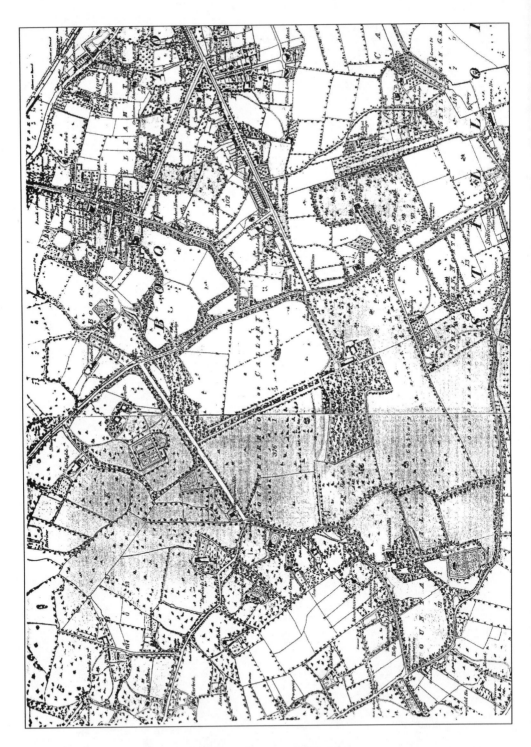

Ordnance Survey, 1837 (TC)

26

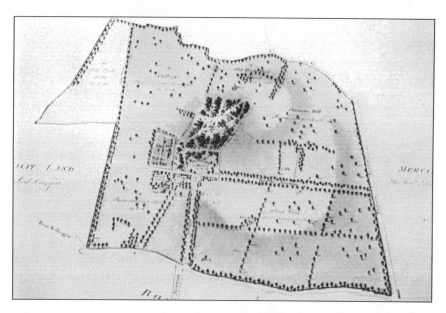

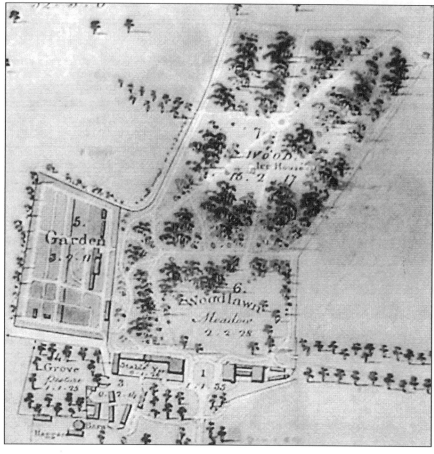

1831 Demesne. House on right, stables on left. (NA1, Pembroke Estate, 2011/2/5)

27

The Pembrokes operated the Mount Merrion demesne as a business, although were frequently at a loss, as illustrated by the Statement of Accounts for 1897:

Receipts		Payments	
Letting of house	£672	Rates, etc.	£458
Grazing, and sale of hay	£1,407	Staff, and estate maintenance	£2,218
Sale of fruit and vegetables, and timber (trees)	£404	Pensions	£66
Loss	£277	Miscellaneous	£18
Total	**£2,760**	**Total**	**£2,760**

Some idea of the letting arrangements for the house can be gleaned from a one year lease, dated 9th December 1898, between Gertrude, Countess of Pembroke, and Thomas Talbot Power. The tenant rented the furnished house and a field known as Donnelly's Park, for £500 for the year. The Pembrokes maintained the outside of the house, in addition to the garden and grounds, and the tenant had a right to walk in the garden and grounds, and to purchase garden produce at market prices. The letting included the coach-house and stables in the Upper Yard, but not the farm stables and out-offices in the Lower Yard (farm-yard). The tenant was allowed to take water from the pump in the field adjoining Donnelly's field. The tenant undertook to give up possession of the premises for any one calendar month during the summer, except the Horse Show Week, without any reduction in rent. Thomas Talbot Power asked for two new baths to be installed, with hot and cold water, (one on ground floor, and another on first floor) in the south wing of the house, and plumbed back to a new range in the first floor kitchen in the rear wing, to which he contributed £50. He continued to rent for a few more years, at a lower rent, before buying the adjoining Thornhill House.

A letter dated 1913 records the following outdoor staff: five men and a boy in the garden and demesne, four men in the pleasure grounds/mowing, two men carting, one carpenter, one general labourer, and the Steward (Mr Crawford). Crawford received £100 per annum, while the rest of the staff shared £561 12s between them for the year. There was also a tradition of giving jerseys or boots to the men each Christmas.

When Lady Beatrix Pembroke was in residence in Mount Merrion in 1914, in company with her two maids, she ordered the following: 30 tons of Wigan coal, for the garden, steward and cottages, 12 tons of coal for the kitchen and ordinary use, and 8 tons of Orrell coal for the sittingrooms.

In 1910/1911, the accounts for the demesne were as follows, when the Pembrokes occupied the house, and therefore, there was no rent:

Receipts		Payments	
Grazing rents	£477	Rates, etc.	£205
Sale of fruit and vegetables	£51	Insurance	£31
Sale of milk	3s 9d	Garden & demesne maintenance	£1,050
Sale of timber	4s 10d	House maintenance	£416
Sale of two cows	£26	Maid's wages	£73
		Phone	£11
		Coal/coke	£62
		Gas	£15
		Chimney (sweep)	£4
		Pensions	£56
Loss	£1,368		
Total	**£1,923**	**Total**	**£1,923**

Lady Beatrix's husband, Sir Neville Wilkinson, achieved some fame for the large doll's house which he commissioned, at enormous expense, called Titania's Palace, which was assembled in the first floor room of the block on the north side of the stables.

During the First World War (1914 – 1918), part of the land nearest the present Lower Kilmacud Road was leased to the British Army as a training ground for recruits.

Sale of Estate

On 1st April 1916, James Adam & Sons, Auctioneers, were commissioned to value the property for the purpose of selling it, and their report makes very interesting reading:

The Mansion House consisted of two distinct buildings, joined together by a two storey structure, built upon arches, spanning an open courtyard, containing the following rooms:

Front Wing
9 foot wide hall, drawing room, dining room, study, all on ground floor.
4 bedrooms, a dressing room and bathroom on the first floor.

Rear Wing
Large sitting room, housekeeper's room (formally a billiard room), kitchen, scullery, larder, dairy, all on ground floor.
4 family bedrooms on first floor.
4 servant's bedrooms in attic.

Link
Butler's pantry and servant's bedroom on lower floor.
2 servant's bedrooms and bathroom on upper floor.

The auctioneer makes a vague mention of the front basement, but did not mention the rear basement, nor are room dimensions given. However, some idea of the room sizes can be gauged from a letter dated 1891, in relation to wallpapering the main rooms, when the following dimensions were given:

Drawing room	97 ft circumference, and 12 ft high
Study	81 ft circumference and 11 ft high
Dining room	96 ft circumference and 11 ft 6 ins high
Study bedroom	78 ft circumference and 9 ft. high
Bedroom over diningroom	96 ft. circumference and 10 ft. high

The heights given may not be the actual heights of rooms, since it was normal for a plain painted frieze to be left along the top of walls.

The stables contained coach houses, stables, laundry, and men's dwellings.

The farm buildings included stable, cart shed, shed, cow shed, stewards cow house, detached carpenter's building, bothy.

There were three gate lodges, a steward's house near the garden, and two workmen's dwellings on Callary Road (now called Lower Kilmacud Road).

The buildings in the walled garden included a melon pit of brick, timber and glass, a 100 ft long peach house, a 100 ft long vinery, and a cucumber pit.

The entire estate was surrounded by a stone wall, 10 ft. high.

By deed dated 13th December 1918, the Earl of Pembroke sold the house and estate of 298 acres to Thomas Joseph O'Neill for £28,500. He in turn sold it on to Thomas Wilson for £36,000 by deed dated 3rd February 1919. By 1928, Wilson sold the property to Mount Merrion Estates Ltd. for £15,000 plus charges of £21,000 (presumably a mortgage). By 1933, Irish Homes Ltd. had acquired the estate, and so began the era of the "Kenny Built" Garden City, so much beloved of auctioneers thereafter.

Preparations for the sale of the property produced many lists and inventories, including the quantity of timber on the estate – 617 beech trees, 156 ash, 550 oak, 573 elm, 157 chestnut, 457 sycamore, 257 fir, 14 larch and 8 lime. In the Deer Park, there were 29 fallow deer (22 does and 7 bucks). Two live does and one buck were packed in crates and shipped across the Irish Sea to England, and amazingly, arrived safely in Wilton House, Salisbury, in 1918. It seems that the remaining deer might have been allowed to roam free on the estate or partly on the adjoining Mount Anville estate, although they may have been caught and transported elsewhere.

♣

The parish priest demolished the splendid and historic original house in 1976, leaving only the poor 1760's extension, which is now used as part of the Community Centre. The 1711 datestone is a recent addition, and comes from the original building, on the site of the present church.

Nowadays there are plenty of physical reminders of the Fitzwilliam demesne, including the old part of the present Community Centre opposite the Church of St. Therese (only the four external walls were retained in the recent refurbishment, losing the entire roof, floors, partitions, windows, etc), most of the old stables at 93, The Rise, the chief steward's house at 29 Trees Road (behind modern houses), the high brick wall of the former gardens, which now separates gardens on The Rise and Trees Avenue, a pair of two storey workman's houses at the corner of Redesdale Road and Lower Kilmacud Road, and a single storey lodge at the corner of Deerpark Road and Mount Anville

Road, the latter two bearing the logo of the Pembrokes – the interwoven letters EPM, signifying the Earl of Pembroke and Montgomery. Only the lodge logo includes the crown above it. In places, old stone boundary walls can be seen. Up until the 1970's, there was a lodge to the south of the present Esso petrol station on the Stillorgan Road, serving the Common Road up to the farmyard. The wedge of land between the Common Road and the East Avenue (main avenue) was called The Shoulder of Mutton Field!

Some people think that the main East Avenue extended from Blackrock right up to the house, but Mount Merrion Avenue was not laid out until the 1750's, some decades after the demesne was created, and is slightly offset where it meets the Stillorgan Road, presumably to prevent any coach and horses galloping straight through the junction!

In 1865, there was an interesting proposal to build a railway through part of the Fitzwilliam estate, including a tunnel connecting Foster Avenue with Mount Merrion Avenue, but nothing came to pass.

Over the years, various documents referred to a Right of Way enjoyed by the Fitzwilliams over the land of the adjoining Thornhill House, via Callary Lane, and the lane is still visible today, although overgrown, along the north side of Oatlands College playing field, leading to the new monastery.

North elevation of the former stables, in 1957.
Espoir Youth Club was on 1st floor. (Irish Independent)

32

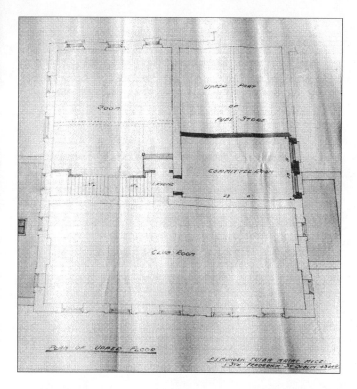

Former stables. Now site of Scouts Hall. Part of rear wall is still standing. (IAA)

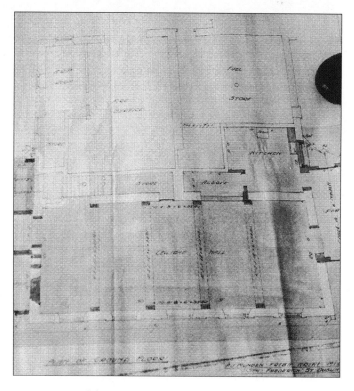

East side of old house in 1970's: Chapel on left, curates quarters overhead, Primary School on right. (KH)

West side in 1970's School on left, chapel on right. (KH)

1960's: Mount Merrion House on front right, former stables on front left. (Aerofilms)

1970's Aerial. (SST)

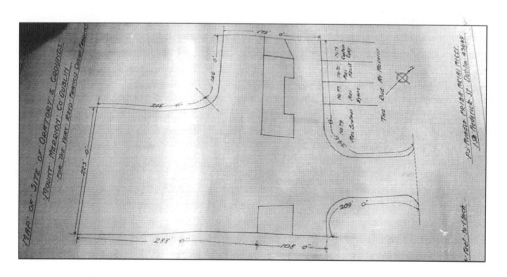

Initial land acquisition by Church – the present Rise is on the right (IAA)

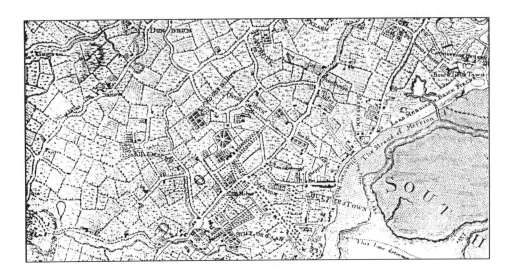

Rocque 1760. (TC)

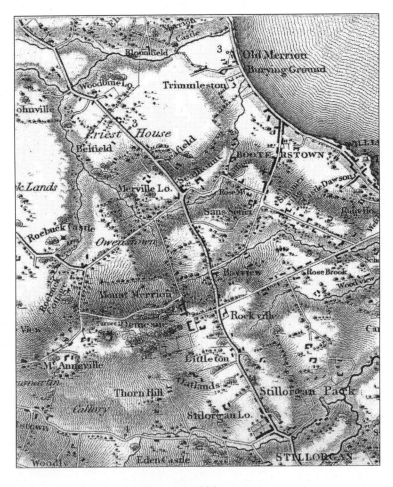

Duncan 1821. (TC)

36

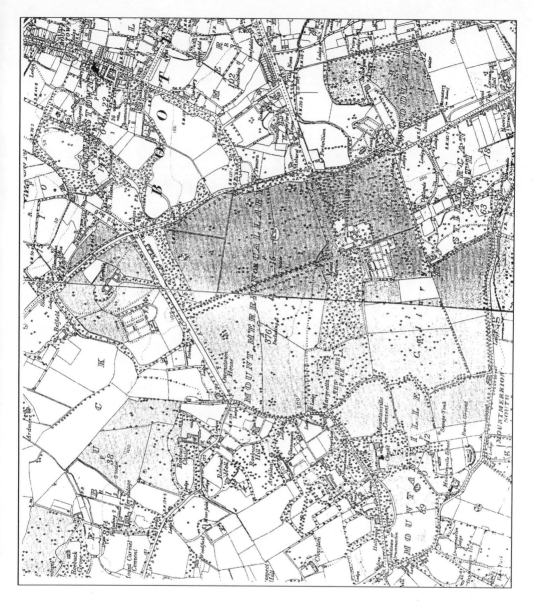

Ordnance Survey, 1907. (TC)

1981 photo of lodge beside Esso garage on N11. (Anon)

37

Lodge at 1 Deerpark Road

Two workers houses on Kilmacud Road

**1890's Stewards House at 29 Trees Road.
The original house was L-shaped.
Various extensions have been added.**

Chapter 2

CHURCH OF ST. THERESE

In 1787, Booterstown, Blackrock, Stillorgan and Dundrum were made into one parish, following a separation from Donnybrook (which also included Ballsbridge, Ringsend and Irishtown). There was only one chapel to serve this large area, located in Booterstown Ave, having been built around 1697. By 1812, a new chapel was built on the same site, at the sole expense of Lord Fitzwilliam (although by now the family were Protestants), largely at the request of the family agent, Mrs. Barbara Verschoyle, who was a Catholic. A Chapel-of-Ease was built in Dundrum in the 1820/30's, to make it easier for parishioners in that part of the parish to attend Mass. Another Chapel of Ease was provided in 1867 in Kilmacud to serve the village of Stillorgan and Kilmacud, and named after Saints Laurence and Cuthbert. This chapel was in fact a converted section of the 1840's National School, because pupil numbers had fallen after the Ladies of Mount Anville opened a National School further up the road towards Goatstown, in 1866. A new curates house was built alongside the Kilmacud chapel-of-ease. Dundrum church was rebuilt in 1879, at which stage Dundrum and Kilmacud split from Booterstown to became a separate parish.

The Fitzwilliam residence, Mount Merrion House, was sold in 1918, but house building only took off in 1933, when Irish Homes Ltd. started developing their "garden city" under John Kenny Builders. Irish Homes Ltd. sold the old mansion and some land to Archbishop Byrne in 1935, for £2,000, on a 900 year lease, at a ground rent of 1s a year. This was a bargain price, since Adams Auctioneers had valued the house alone in 1916 at £3,600. Nowadays, all church property is held by the St Laurence O'Toole Diocesan Trust. Fr. Farrington, the parish priest of Dundrum and Kilmacud, was entrusted with the task of providing a Chapel-of-Ease in Mount Merrion. Using the south block of the old house (1760's), he extended and converted the ground floor into a homely chapel, and used the first floor as the curate's residence. The rest of the old house (north block) was converted into a National School in 1939 (see later Chapter). In 1948, the Chapel-of-Ease separated from Dundrum Parish, and was formed into the new parish of Mount Merrion and Kilmacud. A site at the corner of the Stillorgan Road and Sycamore Crescent was initially chosen for a new church, but eventually the hill site to the west of the old mansion was chosen. "Woodville" was later built by Sharpe on the Sycamore site.

1953 saw the laying of the foundation stone for the new church, which was completed by February 1956, and dedicated to St Therese of the Infant Jesus.

Architect John Robinson (now the practice of Robinson Keefe and Devane) designed the church, and John Philip du Moulin Ltd. built it, after a giant redwood tree was cut down, although one beauty still remains near the south side of the church.

The main walls are of reinforced concrete, faced with chiselled ashlar granite from County Dublin, and Ballinasloe limestone dressings around the windows, and to the portico at the rear, all drylined with plasterboard on timber battens internally. The double pitched roof comprises steel trusses supporting timber rafters and timber boarding, and covered with green Westmoreland slates. A tower/belfry is attached to the north east corner, complete with copper cupola and rope operated bell. The 25 cwt. (hundredweight) bronze bell was cast in 1954 in the Matthew O'Byrne bell foundry (also called the Fountain Head Bell Foundry) in 42, James' Street. The Latin inscriptions on the exterior of the bell refer to Archbishop McQuaid of Dublin and Fr. Deery, the parish priest. The bell was abandoned in 1984, in favour of a recording, via amplifiers, mounted in the cupola, but nothing beats the mature tone of a real bell. The confession boxes project externally, so as to provide a flush wall inside the church. The ceiling of the church is a segmental shape, and plastered to give a coffered appearance, with lights sunk into the coffers. The ceiling rises in a slight dome shape over the crossing of the nave and transepts, and the words "Matthew, Mark, Luke and John" are a feature of the corners. The famous firm of M. Creedon Ltd. was responsible for all the plasterwork. A novel feature for the 1950's was the heated concrete floor throughout the church, with hot water flowing through embedded steel pipes, all powered by an oil fired boiler. The concrete floor was then covered with asphalt and decorative rubber in the circulation areas, and hardwood woodblock flooring in the seating areas. John du Moulin was the first church builder in Ireland to use a Liebher tower crane.

The teak seating/benches were made by Gillian & Co. of Kilmainham. A rear balcony was provided, but no organ. There are 17 ft. diameter limestone rose windows in the rear and the two transepts, while the nave windows feature leadwork and lightly coloured glass, in contrast to the dark green glass used for the cross in each window.

The artist, Sean Keating, was responsible for the painting of St. Therese in a side alter off the west transept, consisting of two panels of hardboard. Sean is better known for his paintings of the men from the Aran Islands, and the construction of the first ESB hydropower station at Ardnacrusha, in Co. Limerick. Another artist, George Collie, painted the Stations of the Cross.

The basic building cost £139,000, which was partly donated by people from all over Ireland, who were asked to sponsor each stone. Another £60,000 was spent on seats, altars, statues, etc., bringing the total to around £200,000. Mortgages were unheard of in those days, so the parishioners spent many years fundraising by means of garden fetes, concerts, etc. The annual Mount Merrion Horse Show in St Helens (CBS) was great fun, and raised some funds.

In the early 1940's, Fr. Farrington had plans to convert part of the old stables into a Ceili Hall/Parish Hall. This imposing building was at the north end of the stables, facing the main mansion house, while the rest of the stables was of a different design, and owned by builder, John du Moulin. The Ceili Hall was intended to be on the ground floor of the building, but in fact, a ballroom was provided on the first floor. The Espoir Youth Club was started by teenagers in January 1957 in a barn attached to Cosgrave's farm on Roebuck Road. When the parish priest heard about the youth club, he immediately offered the teenagers space in the Stables/Parish Hall, but the name "The Barn" still stuck. Their first dance here was held in August 1957. Teenagers for miles around would flock to this venue for dances, etc. The Barn was condemned in 1961, and the Espoir Club moved across into the former chapel-of-ease, still calling it the Barn. The old and new Barn was the venue for many concerts, dances and clubs over the years, with the proceeds going to the church building fund. There was even a Musical Society and a canoeing club.

The old ballroom beside the stables was abandoned, and caught fire in 1968, after which it was demolished, and in 1976, the Scouts built their den on the site, and this building is still being used by the Boys Scouts and the Girl Guides. However, part of the old rear wall is still standing, comprising lovely rubble granite, and cut limestone dressings.

In 1979, the New Barn was abandoned in favour of a newly built community centre, where teenage discos were held.

In 1989, the north carpark was jointly developed with the County Council, reflecting the increased use of motor vehicles to get to church.

By 2003, the historic old section of the Community Centre (part of the Fitzwilliam mansion) was substantially rebuilt (except for the four main walls, and a brick vaulted wine cellar), and a new block built to link the 1979 community hall to the old section. Surprisingly, none of the present windows face towards Dublin Bay, thereby depriving users of wonderful views. Nowadays various rooms in the community centre are hired out to a myriad of clubs from all over Dublin, and the new basement is hired out as a crèche. On Sundays, the centre is closed.

To mark the silver jubilee of the church in 1981, the altar was replaced and turned around, to reflect the new Catholic doctrine. The Golden Jubilee of the church was celebrated in 2006 by expending nearly €2 million on redecorating, refurbishing, and forming a large Baptism and standing area at the rear. The project involved the total removal of the concrete floor, and installing new underfloor heating. During this seven month project, Mass was held in the Community Centre hall on weekdays, and in the nearby Scoil San Treasa Hall on Sundays. In conjunction with the refurbishment, the Parish Priest was granted a Coat of Arms by the Chief Herald of Ireland, with the motto, In Corde Ecclesiae Amor.

Church during construction (Biotrin)

John Du Moulin on left. (Biotrin)

Church in 2007

2007 Refurbished church.

2003 altered/refurbished Community Centre.
The right part was the 1930's chapel (the 1760's extension on the original mansion).

Former stables (now Biotrin), looking south.

Former stables now occupied by Biotrin, and owned by Du Moulin. The boundary wall on the right is the remains of The Barn, with modern Scouts Hall behind

Aerial view in early 1950's. (NL)

Kilmacud split from Mount Merrion to become a separate parish in 1964, and they built their new church in 1969, named after Saint Laurence O'Toole. Their former Chapel of Ease, which was extended over the years, was converted into a fruit shop and a drapery shop, both of which are still going strong, while the adjoining curate's house is now a Scouts Den.

45

Chapter 3

SCOIL SAN TREASA

Irish Homes Ltd/John Kenny Builders started house building activities in 1933, and they set up a Junior and Kindergarten School in No. 20, Greenfield Road, which opened in September 1935, run by Miss E. Peet and Miss D. Baskin.

After the Parish Priest of Dundrum purchased Mount Merrion House in 1935, he resolved to set up a small primary school in the north wing of the old mansion house. The south wing of the old mansion was converted in 1935/1936 into a Chapel-of-Ease, with curate's residence directly overhead on the first floor. By 1939, the architects, P.J. Munden, had been commissioned to turn the four first floor rooms into three classrooms and a teacher's room, and part of the ground floor into separate boy's and girl's cloakrooms and toilets, disregarding the basement and attic rooms. Classes A and B were intended for 30 pupils each, while Class C was for 36 pupils. Obviously the initial intake of children was much smaller, and in fact, catered for all denominations, under the Principal, Mrs. Moran.

One of the teachers who taught in the school from around 1950 to 1970 was the well liked Emily O'Donovan (nee O'Brien), who previously taught in the Loreto Convent, St. Stephens Green. Some of her training copybooks and early time tables from the Loreto days have survived, and we presume that the curriculum was no different when she moved to Mount Merrion. The main subjects for the younger pupils were Gaeilge, Bearla, agus Aireamh (Irish, English and Arithmetic), and apparently in the early days, all subjects were taught through the medium of Irish. Stories, poems and songs included in the children's education included She is Far from the Land, a Celtic Lullaby, A Cradle Song, Bird's Song at Eventide, and a few religious songs were also included, such as Tantum Ergo, Adoremus and O'Salutaris. The 6th Class learned History, Geography, Gaeilge, English, Arithmetic, Algebra and Sewing.

Mount Merrion and Kilmacud became a separate parish in 1948, and built the new Church of St. Therese in 1956.

Within a few years, the decision was taken to build a new primary school to cater for the additional houses built in Mount Merrion in the post war years. The new school opened in 1963, with hall and two storey class block facing the back wall of the church, and a two storey service block linked to a single storey west classroom block beside North Avenue.

Initially the school was for girls only, but went co-educational in the 1980's. The prefabs alongside the church are there since 1995, and are used by Low and High Infants (boys and girls). Coincidentally, that was the same year that the first male principal was appointed. Internally the school has a bright and welcoming atmosphere, with plenty of children's artwork adorning the classrooms and corridors. The school now has 445 pupils, a Principal, 22 teachers, and 9 special needs assistants (engaging on a one-to-one basis). A recent innovation is an Interactive Whiteboard, computer linked, which is a far cry from the days of blackboards, chalk, and dusters!

Side of present school near Trees Avenue.

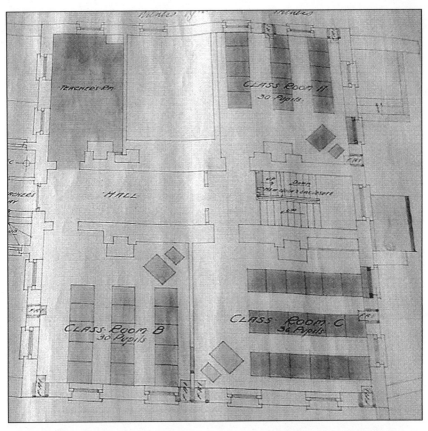

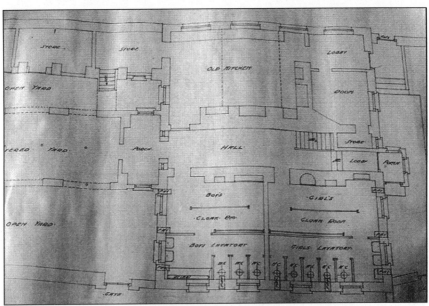

**Top: First floor classrooms in Mount Merrion House
Bottom: Ground floor cloakrooms. (IAA)**

An tSeachtain dár chríoch 1ad M.F. '39.

Gaedhilg Léigheann, litriú, leac 3 7 4.
——— Cómhrádh
  (a) Is, 'seadh, ní h-eadh.
  (b) An Caisleán féin.
  (c) Sgéal: Seán 7 an Leipreachán.
  Scríobhadh : cinn línte ; ath-sgríobhadh.

Béarla Reading, Spelling and Explanation
——— Reader. Page 13, 14.
  Writing : Headlines, Transcription,
  Word - Building.

Áireamh Cleachtadh ar suimiú 7 dealú. *
——— Táible Méaduighthe a cheartú.
  Obair béil. Fadhbanna simplidhe.

* 75 +57

$$75 \atop 57 \atop \overline{132}$$ $$75 \atop 57 \atop \overline{18}$$ $$132 \atop 18 \atop \overline{114}$$. Fr. 114.

Clár Ama.

	Dia luain	D. Máirt	D. Céadaoin	Dardaoin	D. ah-Aoine
9.30 – 10	Gaedhilg	Gaedhilg	Gaedhilg	Gaedhilg	Gaedhilg.
10 – 10.30	"	"	"	"	"
10.30 – 11	Áireamh		Composition	Áireamhaidheacht	Áireamh
11 – 11.30	"	English	"	Áireamh	"
11.30 – 12		Teagasg Críosraidhe			
12 – 12.30			Sos.		
12.30 – 1	History	O. Snáraidhe	Geography	Algéabar	Gaedhilg.
1 – 1.30	"	"	"	History	
1.30 – 2	Algéabar.	Áireamh	Scríobh English	Áireamh	English
2 – 2.30	English.	History	History	English	History
2.30 – 3	Geography. [Eolas ar Nádúr]	Geography	Algéabar.	Grammar	Algéabar

1930's Timetable and syllabus for Loreto Primary School (same as Scoil San Treasa?).

Chapter 4

DEERPARK

The biggest attraction in Mount Merrion is the wonderful County Council Park, extending to about 34 acres, and commanding a fantastic view of Dublin City and Bay from its vantage point of 265 feet above sea level. On a clear day, you can see as far as the Ballymun apartment blocks (now nearly all demolished) on the north side of Dublin. On most days you can see the ships gliding in and out of Dublin Port, beneath the landmark twin Pigeon House chimney towers.

The park owes its origin to two neighbouring demesnes, those of Fitzwilliam/Pembroke, and Mount Anville Convent, the former being represented by the wood and land as far as the Mount Anville Road entrance, and the latter comprising the open area alongside Mount Anville Park housing estate. In fact the diagonal path which connects the Mount Anville Road gate with the Redesdale Road gate represents the old boundary wall between the two estates.

The wood in the Fitzwilliam section of the park corresponds exactly with the wood shown on all the estate maps back to at least the early 18th century. Cullen's map of 1722 refers to Woodhill, and Barkers map of 1762 specifically shows the wood, with a gazebo near the west end, and 32 paths radiating from there. A painting by William Ashford in 1806 shows the same arrangement. By 1831, the wood is shown as more informal, with only 5 radiating paths. The large area between the mansion house and the wood is marked as Woodlawn, and this is where the present St. Therese Church and Scoil San Treasa Primary School were built in the 1950/60's.

After the First World War, the Mount Merrion demesne was sold to developers, but it lay idle for many years. The Housing Corporation of Great Britain Ltd designed a grand housing scheme to be known as Mount Merrion Park, which envisaged most of the new houses being built in the east half of the estate, retaining the wood and west part of the estate for a golf course. In later decades, the golf course idea was exchanged for bricks and mortar, leaving only the woods and the field to the west of it, and the latter two areas were effectively abandoned, and became the unofficial playground for the children of the new housing estate.

By the late 1950's, Dublin County Council decided to acquire the land by Compulsory Purchase, and an arbitrator was appointed to assess compensation, holding public hearings in 1961 and 1962. Hence 24 acres was acquired from Wilson and Maher via this process, for £6,250, and similarly with a one acre plot which the Smurfit family owned. By 1971, the Council could effectively declare the public park open.

The late 1970's saw Mount Anville convent selling off the farm portion of their 90-acre estate, resulting in the construction of houses in Mount Anville Wood and Mount Anville Park. A condition of the Planning Permission stipulated that 7 acres of open space be allocated for the new residents. Quite sensibly, this was positioned alongside the recently opened Deerpark, and by demolishing the separating wall, a much larger public park emerged.

Only in 1998 was the final piece of the park acquired by the Council, for £15,000, and this is now the site of the recently opened children's playground. This small plot belonged to David Whitren, who originally had planned to build his Stella ballroom here, but opted instead for the site across the road (the present Kiely's pub).

And the burning question – why is the park called Deerpark? Because the Fitzwilliams/Pembrokes called it so, and in fact kept their herd of deer here. In the 19th century, it was fashionable for all the "big houses" to have a deer park, usually for the sport of stag-hunting, but also as "window dressing", and sometimes for a supply of tasty meat. Sometimes deer were stored on smaller estates, and later transported and released for a big hunt, such as the Ward Union Hunt in north County Dublin. The 1831 estate map shows a Sunk Fence between the old Deer Park (the field to the west of the wood) and the larger northern portion of the estate, and this was a step in the land, in order to contain the deer. This arrangement is called a "ha-ha", which is the term used to describe a sunken road or path (usually 2 metres below ground level), to enable vehicles and people to pass in front of the main house, to and from stables, farmyard, etc., without being seen by the gentry inside, or perhaps spoiling a vista. Nowadays part of the Sunken Fence can be seen in the lane behind the shops on Deerpark Road, comprising a low section of stone retaining wall. When Mount Merrion demesne was sold in 1918 to developers, three of the fallow deer were shipped live in crates to the Pembroke main estate in England (and arrived safely!) It seems that the remaining 26 deer were left to run wild on the estate, although other big houses or hunts may have taken them away. Nowadays the only wildlife in the woods is a family of grey squirrels, although these have the potential to strip the bark from trees, and so kill the trees.

Other remnants of the old demesne which the local children enjoyed for decades were the Ice House near the east side of the wood, and the cold water storage cistern on the west side of the wood. The former was a stone or brick lined underground room, used to store perishable food in the days before the refrigerator, and the latter would have supplied the house and farmyard with water – the elevated location of the tank relative to the house would have provided good pressure. These are now long gone.

In 1976, the Deer Park Tennis Club was founded by Dick Humphreys, utilising the four tennis courts which had already been built by the County Council. Shortly after this, the Council entered into a yearly Management Licence with the first Trustees of the club: Canon James Ardle Mac Mahon, Canon Trevor S. Hipwell, and Rev. Desmond Black - the Catholic, Anglican, and Presbyterian clergy. 10-years later they built their clubhouse and four floodlit all-weather courts, mostly funded by the County Council/FAS. In recent years, two other fenced courts were built, a short distance from the main courts and clubhouse. In 2010, the National Lottery funded an extension to the tennis clubhouse, including an attic conversion. Nowadays, the Management Licence is for 10 years from 2007, at a nominal yearly rent of €100, and the present Trustees are: Colin Motyer, Cosmo Flood, Conor Gunne, and Liam Prendiville. Unfortunately, the tennis courts and clubhouse are very much under-used by the young people of Mount Merrion, because of the misconception that it is a private tennis club. However, it should be remembered that the Management Licence stipulates: "Except during the playing of certain pre-arranged tournaments, championship and league matches etc, the Club shall ensure that one court be nominated and made available on a first come, first served basis to persons who are not members of the Club". €5 (€10 for two), is the current rate for non-members.

In 1974, the Mount Merrion Youths Football Club (Soccer) was founded, and is still going strong, playing regularly on the west side of the tennis courts. In the 1990's they built the western section of the tennis clubhouse. There are also two Gaelic football pitches in the park, sometimes used by Kilmacud Crokes, although they have their own grounds beside Glenalbyn Swimming Pool. They now use the middle section of the present tennis clubhouse.

It wasn't until Spring 2006 that the Council decided to build a children's playground, opposite Kiely's pub on Deerpark Road, and this very colourful and cosy area, set amidst mature trees, is like a magnet to youngsters and grown up children. The swinging basket seems to get the most use.

Nowadays the woods contain mostly oak, beech and chestnut, although there are examples of many other species. Quite a number of the original trees have been blown down or uprooted in storms, especially in the 2006/2007 Winter, but the Council has planted various other trees, to provide a well balanced environment. They also planted a small number of trees in random parts of the playing pitches. Tarmac paths now run around the complete perimeter of the park, in addition to a few internal paths, all of which are pounded daily by strollers and joggers. A few wooden benches are scattered around the park.

2006 Aerial view looking east. (PB)

Ashford colour painting, 1805 (FM)

53

New playground, with Flanagans Furniture in background.

Tennis clubhouse in 2010 (right part only). Middle part is used by
Kilmacud Crokes, and left part by Mount Merrion Youth Football Club

2010 photo of soccer match.

1850's Valuation Office map, showing various estates and parcels of land. (VO)

Chapter 5

MOUNT MERRION PARK HOUSING ESTATE

In the eyes of many auctioneers, Mount Merrion houses mean "Kenny Built", whereas John Kenny was responsible for less than half the houses in the current Mount Merrion neighbourhood.

Thomas Joseph O'Neill bought the original 300-acre demesne from the Pembroke family in 1918, for £28,500, and sold it on the following year to Thomas John Wilson for £36,000. Presumably because of the War of Independence, and subsequent Civil War, it wasn't until the mid 1920's that sites were sold to small builders, and some bungalows were built on Mount Anville Road (roughly opposite the present Council Depot), Roebuck Avenue, Foster Avenue and St. Thomas Road, but sales were slow. In 1928, Wilson sold the demesne to Mount Merrion Estates Ltd. for £15,000 plus £21,000 in charges (presumably a mortgage), and they appointed the Housing Corporation of Great Britain Ltd. to produce a masterplan for the entire estate (renamed Mount Merrion Park), and this envisaged housing on the eastern half, and a golf course on the western half with the woods as a centerpiece. A marketing suite was set up in the north block of the stables, and the promotional brochure included the timetables for two bus services, one the United Tramways Co. Ltd., to/from O'Connell Bridge, Dun Laoghaire, and Bray, and the Robin Bus Co. to/from Burgh Quay and Foxrock. In the same year, Mount Merrion Estates Ltd. reached an agreement with Rathdown No. 1 Rural District Council in relation to the provision of public sewers. In those days, Mount Merrion was also called Callary, and was located in the Half Barony of Rathdown, Co. Dublin. However, it wasn't until Irish Homes Ltd. appointed John Kenny & Sons as builders in 1933, that the estate began to develop in earnest. John Kenny demolished the high stone wall, which surrounded the demesne, excluding the four stone pillars and cast iron gates and railings opposite the top of Mount Merrion Avenue. Around this time, Willow Park Junior School opened, as part of Blackrock College, and in the 1940's the piers and gates were re-assembled as their main entrance off the Rock Road, after the Holy Ghost fathers bought the gates at auction. One of the granite balls was left behind, and now sits in the side garden of Sycamore Lodge. One wonders what became of the splendid cast-iron gates leading into the Rose Walk. The acquisition of the pillars and gates by Blackrock College was a potent gesture, to mark the purchase in 1938 by the Holy Ghost Order of the freehold to their land, which was only held on lease from the Fitzwilliams/Pembroke Estate, ever since the

College opened in 1860. Willow Park was owned by the famous Bewley family, and was sold to the priests in 1924, for use as their seminary. When the seminary moved to Kimmage Manor in 1936, the building was converted for use as the Junior School for Blackrock College.

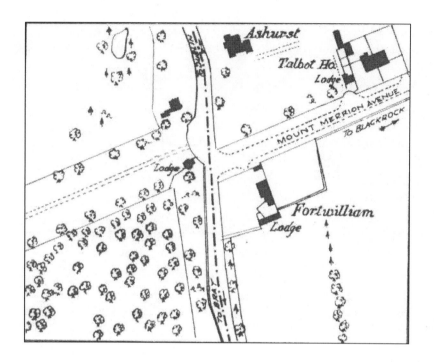

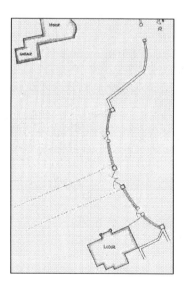

Two 1934 maps of entrance. (ESB)

Kenny completed the first pair of houses in 1934 (Nos. 1 and 3 Greenfield Road), proceeding to Sycamore Road, The Rise, Greygates, Trees Road Lower, The Close, Chestnut Road, over the next 5-years. The few shops on the Rise were built in this period, and also Estate Garage Ltd. (1936) on the Stillorgan Road, including a sweet shop and vegetable shop (now the Esso Garage). Sycamore Lodge was the work of another builder after the War, and the owners sold off part of their side garden in 1970, where a smaller house was built, and later re-modeled and extended.

Irish Homes Ltd. and its architect, Rupert Jones, knew that their houses would have to be special, in order to attract buyers to this semi rural location. They prepared a new estate plan, retained as many of the mature trees as possible, laid out very wide roads, provided long back and front gardens, and built a mix of three and four bedroomed houses. Some houses incorporated garages, or alternatively, space at the side was left for a future garage. The promotional brochure boasted of a minimum of 110 ft between the front of opposite houses, six houses to the acre, and 50 different house types. Most important of all, no two pairs of houses were exactly the same. Various little architectural features on different houses added diversity and interest, such as some half timbered facades, bay or bow windows, recessed porches (some arched), recessed balconies, overhanging eaves, gable hip roofs, gambrel roofs, natural slates or plain concrete tiles on the roofs, porthole windows, coloured glass in lead cames in hall doors, red tile window cills or other dressings, etc. The crowning feature is probably the patterned render on the outside of all houses, covered with snow white masonry paint.

The Kenny houses were sold for £750 - £1,150, depending on size and design, and held on 900-year leases, for around £10/£12 per annum ground rent.

Prior to the 1930's, homes were heated by coal fires and lit by gas lamps, and kitchens had gas cookers. Electric lighting in Dublin city was largely confined to street lighting. However, with the founding in the late 1920's of the ESB, and building the Ardnacrusha Hydro-Electric Power Station in Limerick, the "all electric" home was promoted. In Mount Merrion, in 1935, the ESB fitted out a new house as a show house, and this was Cuan na Greine, 38, Greenfield Road, owned by the Dempseys. Some rooms were fitted with built-in electric fires in the bottom of the fireplace opening, while in some others, the electric elements were built into the tiled surround on both sides of the fireplace. In bedrooms, the fireplace opening was tiled over, and incorporated electric elements. Hot water was provided by electric immersion heaters and hot water cylinders. The road immediately to the west of this house was called The Corso, but now comprises a fenced-off green, all part of North Avenue.

Unfortunately, a 6-month strike in the building industry forced work to stop in 1937, and this was followed by the Second World War, during which nothing was built, and so ended Kenny's wonderful work.

After the War, F.W. Wilson, son of the original purchaser of the demesne, and his partner, Mather, developed the Wilson Estate, comprising Deerpark Road, Callary Road, Cypress Road, North Avenue, and of course Wilson and Mather Roads, named after themselves. They employed different builders such as McNeill, Towey, etc. A few houses at the bottom of North Avenue were built by someone else at the start of the War, when certain materials were in short supply. John du Moulin built some houses at the top of The Rise.

The 1950's saw more house building to the south of Deerpark, comprising Trees Road Upper, Redesdale Road, Thornhill Road, Clonmore Road, Cedarmount Road, Glenabbey Road, etc., with different builders being involved.. The bungalows along Kilmacud Road were built at this time, although four two-storey houses near the east end were built in 1932. Most of the post-war housing comprised smaller and less ornate dwellings, more suited to the needs of a depressed economy. Wilson and Mather still retained land after all the foregoing house building, since part of the present Deerpark was Compulsory Purchased from them in the 1960's.

Foster Avenue is the only road which was developed piecemeal from the 1920's to the 1960's, ranging from old bungalows, to the more modern early 1960's dormer-style Wates bungalows in The Fosters and St. Thomas Mead.

In the Kenny part of the estate, a few houses stand out as different, since their design tries to emulate the Modern Movement favoured by French architect, Le Corbusier, sweeping Europe in the 1920's and 30's. Three houses went for a spartan look, with flat roofs, plain painted render, corner suntrap windows, and sometimes very wide windows. "Stanstead", and the house diagonally opposite, at the junction of Greenfield Road and North Avenue, went in for this image, although St. Damiens, a few doors to the north of the Stillorgan Park Hotel, is probably a better example. The County Council planners have listed these three houses as Protected Structures.

The property market boom over the last 10-15 years has led to many people extending their house instead of trading-up. Mount Merrion, in particular, has seen attic conversions, two storey side extensions, rear extensions, and even new houses in side gardens, especially on corner sites. A new trend is the building of habitable basements under new houses. It is probably true to say that the number of habitable rooms in Mount Merrion has increased by at least

10% - the equivalent of one new road! Unfortunately the original architectural ambiance of the neighbourhood is being eroded, especially in the Kenny-built section, which some day may prove to be regrettable.

1 and 3 Greenfield Road

Builder John Kenny on left, and architect Rupert Jones on right.

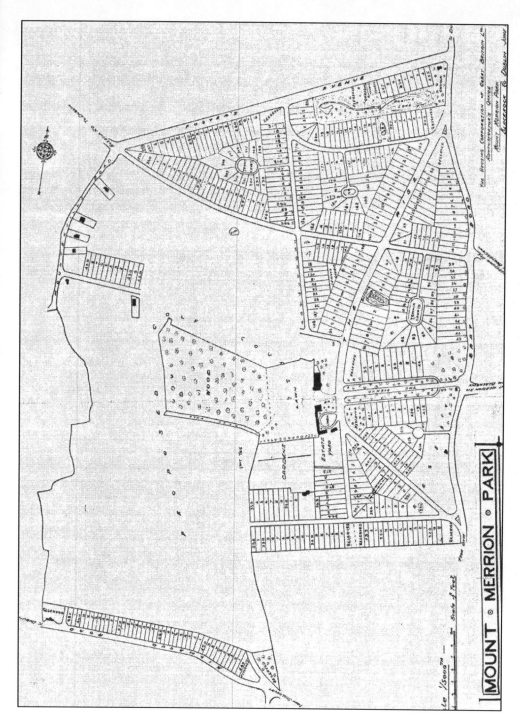

1928 Proposed estate layout (not final layout)

61

Ordnance Survey map: 1936. (TC)

Chapter 6

MOUNT ANVILLE BOARDING SCHOOL

Mount Anville adjoined the west side of Mount Merrion demesne, the property of the Fitzwilliam family. Mount Anville originally was part of the land of Lord Trimleston, and in the townland of Roebuck. When Lord Trimleston surveyed his property in 1783, Mount Anville demesne was smaller, amounting to 41 acres, shown as plots 1-20 on the map, with plot No 1 representing the house (a small building). Major Butler occupied plots 21-28, and there were at least two small houses on his demesne, including one right alongside the house in Mount Anville. When Lord Fitzwilliam surveyed part of his properties in 1773, Mount Anville house and Major Butlers house are shown as two single-storey dwellings. It is obvious that the two demesnes were combined, and the two small houses demolished to make way for one large house, probably around 1801.

Lewis, writing in 1837, states that Mount Anville is occupied by the Honourable Charles Burton, Second Justice of the Court of Queen's Bench, and remarkable for its richly cultivated gardens and extensive conservatories. From 1839 to 1851, Elizabeth West occupied the property, which included a pleasure ground, ponds, fountains, various lodges, and even a Mass House at the rear, sized 33 ft x 15½ ft x 12½ ft high, and at that stage, a 10 ft. high stone wall surrounded the estate.

From 1851 to 1865, William Dargan, the famous railway contractor, was the owner, and he called the property "The Tower". Dargan was born in 1799 to a small farmer in Co. Carlow, and trained as a surveyor in England, working for the famous iron bridge builder, Thomas Telford. Returning to Ireland, he built Ireland's first passenger railway in 1834, from Dublin to Kingstown (Dun Laoghaire), and went on to build many more railways and canals throughout Ireland. He is credited with creating the Dargan Channel in Belfast Port (also called Victoria Channel), and using the dredged material to form Queens Island, which later became the shipyards of Harland and Wolfe. He became very wealthy, and was able to sponsor the Dublin Industrial Exhibition on Leinster Lawn in 1853, to the tune of £100,000, although lost £20,000 in the process. However, his endeavours in the 1850's to grow flax in Co. Cork, in addition to building the associated linen mills, including one in Chapelizod, Co. Dublin, were not successful, so that he was in financial difficulties in 1865, forcing him to sell his house and farm in Mount Anville. The Valuation Office records in

1864 that the 92 acres were leased from Henry Kemmis, and that the property was "much improved by Mr. Dargan – dwelling enlarged, and new roofs and Tower. A first class mansion and beautiful situation". The Valuation Office also noted that Dargan was selling the property for £35,000 (but eventually only obtained £10,000). Following a horse-riding accident, Dargan died in 1867 at his townhouse, No. 2, Fitzwilliam Square, leaving his widow Jane (nee Haslam?), but no children. In 1864, the new National Gallery erected a statue in his honour on their front lawn, because he was instrumental in founding the gallery, shortly after the Great Exhibition on the adjacent Leinster Lawn.

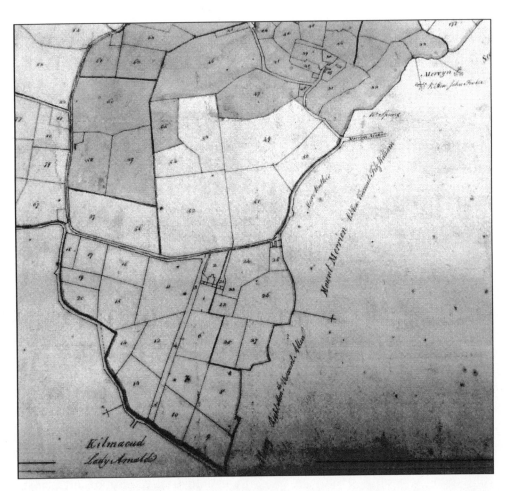

1783 map – Mount Anville is bottom estate (1-20). Roebuck Castle is No 29. All of this land belonged to Lord Trimleston. (NAI, Pembroke Estate)

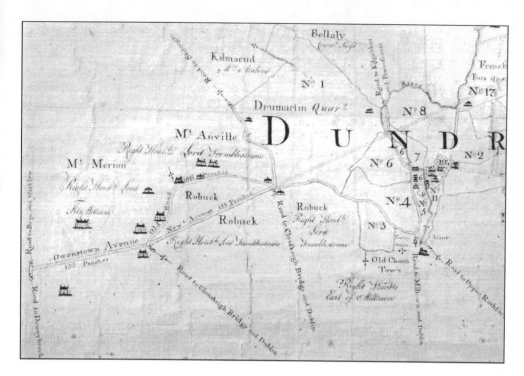

1773 map: Mount Anville is single storey, alongside Major Butler. (NA1, Pembroke Estate)

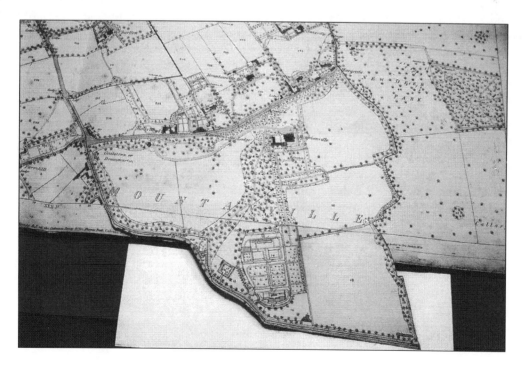

1866 Map. (NA1)

In 2005, Dargan was again honoured when the newly opened cable-stayed Luas railway bridge at Dundrum was named after him. He is still remembered in Bray, for bringing the railway line, building the Promenade, and various other ventures. His flax-spinning mill in Chapelizod was built in 1856 near the Salmon Leap, and was converted into the Phoenix Park Whiskey Distillery in 1878, lasting until 1921.

The Ladies of the Sacred Heart struck a tough deal when they secured Mount Anville in 1865 for the bargain price of £10,000, no doubt assisted by Archbishop Paul Cullen. The deeds list the purchasers as Alexander Bayle of College Green, Anna Butler, Susan Moltau, Anne Murphy, Susan West, Teresa Harrington, Frances Cravin, all of Glasnevin, and Anne Murphy of Roscrea. The lease was for the remainder of 300-years from 1801, with Thomas Kemmis listed as the lessor. The property came fully stocked with herds of cows and sheep, pigs, hens, etc. Where did the nuns get such a large sum of money? All the top positions in the Order were held by ladies who came from wealthy Catholic families, and usually a large dowry of money or property was given to the convent when a daughter took vows, similar to the rural tradition when a dowry was given by a girl's parents when she married. In 1865, the dowry of Sr. Marcella Hynes paid outright for the Mount Anville property. The Sacred Heart nuns were founded in France in 1800, by Madeline Sophie Barat, and spread to Roscrea in Co. Tipperary in 1842, Armagh in 1851, and Glasnevin in 1853. However, the north side of Dublin did not suit the Ladies, so they sold that property to the Holy Faith nuns, and moved to the spectacular setting of Mount Anville in 1865, bringing their 30 girl boarders with them.

Within 3-years, a new rectangular three storey (plus attic) Boarding School had been built, approx. 30 metres distant from the convent, utilizing granite quarried on the farm (the quarry was under the present hockey pitches), at a cost of £10,000. Nowadays this building is recognizable by the clock and gable section in the centre of the south elevation, and copper clad dormer windows. The dormer windows at the front are tiny, maybe for reasons of privacy, whereas the rear ones are larger, and the high attic space was subdivided as rooms for novices. In the centre is an old mechanical chiming clock, with three bronze bells in the louvred belfry projecting through the roof ridge. The bells are inscribed with the maker's name, Sheridan of Church Street, Dublin, and dated 1870. The largest bell, the tenor, also has a motif comprising Irish symbols, such as a round tower, harp, wolfhound, and the words Erin go Brath – Long Live Ireland. The clock was reconstructed in 1922 by Ganter Brothers of South Great Georges Street, but is no longer used, and instead a small electric clock sits behind the skeletal face in the south gable wall. There are many chimneys at roof level, but only a few open fireplaces remain in random classrooms.

The famous architects, Pugin & Ashlin, designed the Boarding School, while the equally famous Meade carried out the building work. A cloister or corridor linked the new Boarding School to the convent building. Within the next few years, additional wings were added to the south-west, south-east, and north-west corners of the original boarding school, the latter containing fourteen small piano-practice rooms.

1865: First group of boarders. (SHN)

Original Boarding School. (SK)

RECREATION ROOM, with doors of the Lady Chapel thrown open,

Original Boarding School. (SK)

Pre-1888 (NL)

Original chapel before extension. (SK)

"Blue Ribbons" (prefects) in 1908. (SHN)

"Make hay, while the sun shines". (SHN)

Other important dates thereafter include:

1869 – Day Boarding School launched (the girls went home at night, but had all their meals in the school).

1889 – The south-east wing of the Boarding School was demolished, and a chapel built, at the expense of the head office in Paris. It was open to the public. The chapel was built at a time when it was partly visible from the road, and so had to be disguised to satisfy the Protestant authorities. Therefore, the chapel is entered at first floor level, so that the overall height matches the adjoining boarding school, and various rooms were provided underneath the chapel. Internally the chapel is plain, although contains some nice stained glass windows, dedicated to different saints. The St. Michael window on the west side of the apse was provided for the centenary in 1900. George Ashlin designed this chapel, and it was built at a cost of £5,800.

1922/23 - The large U-shaped three storey Novitiate was built between the convent and the boarding school, with plastered walls and battlemented parapets. A new semi basement school hall, with two floors of classrooms over, was built at the same time, although the original ornate arch and surrounds to the stage opening were removed at a later date, reducing the grandeur of the stage. The entire was built without an architect or even drawings – the nuns simply told the builder, P.J. O'Grady, what they needed. The end result was that the north façade of the original boarding school was substantially hidden, and the total complex became an architectural disaster. The novitiate was previously in Roehampton, England, but when the English and Scottish Province joined together in 1918, a new novitiate was decided upon for Mount Anville. This novitiate was phased out in the 1970 /1980's.

1939 – The chapel was extended to the south by three bays, and side aisles, supported on arches.

1944 – Fourth storey added to south-west wing (also known as Music House or Angels Wing) after removal of twin pitched slated roof.

1950's – The original cast iron entrance gates, and granite piers, were moved from beside the present granite gate lodge to their present position opposite the convent. However, the original gates are missing, and may have been re-erected at the entrance to one of the nun's houses at 201, Lower Kilmacud Road. Around this time, the County Council widened Mount Anville Road, and the old stone boundary wall was moved and replaced by a modern wall.

1950 – A two storey extension built behind the south west corner of the convent.

1954 – A Montessori School started in one room of the extension behind the convent.

1955 – A Secondary Day School opened (called Mater Admirabilis).

1966 – The boarders and day girls amalgamated.

1981 – Boarding School closed.

1980's – Cedar House Nursing Home opened (later extended).

1987 – Sports Hall built – ultra modern.

2000 – New Montessori School opened near south west corner of convent.

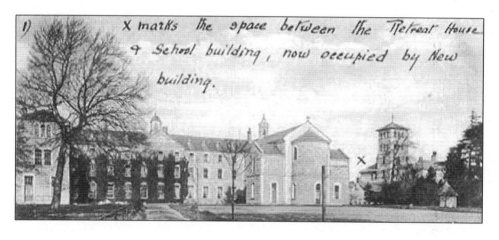

X marks the space between the Retreat House & School building, now occupied by New building.

Pre-1922 postcard, before building of Novitiate at X. (SHN)

The **Census returns for 1901** give a good idea of how Mount Anville was constituted at the turn of the century. There were 85 females residing there, comprising 16 nuns, 15 domestics (servants) and 54 pupils. The word domestic is a misnomer, since these women were in fact novices. 61-year old Helen Roche from Dublin was the head nun, and her colleagues were of different nationalities – 8 Irish, 4 English, 1 Jamaican, 1 German, 1 Belgian and 1 French. All the domestics were Irish. The pupils ranged in age from 11 to 19 (of Secondary School age), with substantial numbers from Dublin and from around the country, in addition to a few from England, two from Jamaica, one from India, and one from France. The premises contained 50 rooms, and had 60 front windows. There were two other small dwellings, one for the steward and his family, and the other for the carpenter's family. The 24 out-offices included three stables, one coachhouse, one harness room, two cow houses, one calf house, one dairy, one piggery, five fowl houses, one barn, one boiler house, one turf house, one potato house, one workshop, one laundry and three stores.

In the **1911 Census**, there were 40 nuns resident and 59 pupils, (of primary and secondary school age). Fifty-nine year old Rose Thunder was the head nun. Later records reveal that about 15 girls were in the Junior School around 1913. Following the construction of a novitiate in 1922-1923, it is probable that many pupils in the school went on to become nuns, and certainly quite a few girls ended up in high positions in the Ladies of the Sacred Heart.

The Catholic Directory records the following information over the decades, although some of these figures may be inaccurate:

1930 – 30 novices, 43 nuns, 60 boarders (obtained from other sources).

1940 – 30 novices, 70 nuns, 120 boarders.

1950 -- 70 nuns, 140 boarders.

1957 -- 67 nuns, 152 boarders, 35 Day Secondary.

1960 -- 68 nuns, 120 boarders, 70 Day Secondary, 100 Montessori.

1970 -- 62 nuns, 130 boarders, 270 Day Secondary, 400 Junior/Montessori.

1980- 42 nuns (plus few outside convent), 540 Day Secondary, 532 Junior/Montessori.

1990 -- 19 nuns (plus others outside), 632 Day Secondary, 453 Junior/Montessori.

2000 -- 20 nuns (plus 20 outside and 44 in Cedar House Nursing Home), 600 Secondary, 240 boys and girls in Montessori.

2006 – 11 nuns in convent (plus 16 outside and 19 in Cedar House), 640 Secondary School plus 55 teachers plus extra staff, 460 Junior/Montessori.

After 1967, when Free Secondary Education was introduced by the Government, the nuns could reduce their fees, since the Government paid the teacher's salaries, and hence student numbers increased. In addition, the closure of the nuns other schools in Lesson Street, Monkstown and Roscrea in the 1960/70's provided a transfer of many pupils to Mount Anville.

Prior to 1931, the boarders did not sit the Leaving Certificate Exam (State run), so could not enter UCD, which in any event was regarded as too rough for the young ladies, and Trinity College was not an option, as it was perceived as being a Protestant institution. So the girls either got married or entered the convent, usually Mount Anville.

Up until 1967, when Free Education was introduced, the nuns were an enclosed order, with strict rules of silence, which were also applied to the boarders. The nuns were not allowed to leave the convent, even for a parent's funeral. In the following decade, the nuns were semi-enclosed, and could go out once or twice a year. The nuns still wore the long black habit, including a type of hoodie, trimmed with white starchy front rim, which prevented them looking sideways. The teaching staff were all nuns, except for one or two lay people. In those days, women teachers had to give up employment as soon as they got married, although this Government rule was lifted in the mid 1970's.

By 1990, the number of girls entering convents had dramatically fallen, and only two nuns were teaching in Mount Anville, and the order was forced to appoint a lay principal.

Mount Anville operated a large farm until the 1970's. The nuns then sought Planning Permission from the County Council for a housing development, but this was only obtained after an Appeal to An Bord Pleanala, and a public oral hearing. 34 acres of development land was then sold to the Gallagher Group in 1977, who built a few hundred houses in Mount Anville Park, Mount Anville Wood, etc., although some other builders were also involved.

One often forgets that nuns adopt a saint's name when they "take the veil", but legally they still retain their maiden names. In this case, the nuns empowered to sell the land were Margaret O'Donoghue, Mary O'Connor, Mary Corless, and Dolores Considine.

The Gallagher Group paid £667,500 (about €850,000), and the nuns used the proceeds for the following purposes:

1.   Purchase of six houses in Mount Anville for nuns - £240,000.
2.   Purchase of two houses on Clonshaugh Road for community work - £30,000
3.   Contribution to Archbishop's Appeal for low priced housing - £40,000
4.   Funds spent on Roscrea Free Education School - £50,000.
5.   Legal Fees - £7,500.
6.   Proposed Nursing Home for nuns (Cedar House) - £300,000.

The locals fought hard to oppose the house building, and Oral Hearings were held by An Bord Pleanala in 1975 and 1977. The open space element of the new housing estate was positioned alongside the recently opened Deerpark, so that once the boundary wall was demolished, the two spaces could be combined into one park (Deerpark).

A smaller parcel of land was sold in 1967, where Mount Anville Lawn houses (nineteen houses) now stand near Drummartin Road. In total, 45 acres were sold over the years, but still leaving 45 acres for the nuns and their school.

The farmyard was at the south centre of the estate, and the main working farm had three large fields – Tower Field at the north (also called Calvary), Hidden Gem in the centre, and Botany Bay at the south (alongside the present Primary School on Kilmacud Road Lower). The Hidden Gem itself was a small wooded area, with a quaint summer house in the centre. The farm also included the 22-acre Lodge Field to the west of the school, but this was not sold – in fact, part has been disused in recent years in case the County Council need to buy it for widening Lower Kilmacud Road (opposite Knocknashee and The Goat Pub).

Originally the nuns enjoyed the ornamental gardens to the south of the convent, but nowadays, tennis courts and Astro-turf all weather hockey pitches occupy the land.

The old house was famous for its grove of Cedar of Lebanon trees to the south west of the building, but these were removed to make way for the Montessori school. The giant redwood tree opposite the convent was planted in 1900 by Queen Victoria of England, not long before her death. She had previously visited in 1853 to offer Dargan a knighthood, but he politely declined.

Single storey Cedar House, which is also listed as 35, Mount Anville Park, is the nuns private nursing home, to the south east of the convent.

The nuns cemetery near the farmyard mostly uses small black cast iron crosses mounted on low headstones, with earlier inscriptions in Latin. The only white marble headstone marks the grave of a pupil, Jeanne de la Touche, who died in 1922, aged 13. The tiny ornate oratory (probably 1870's) was intended as the burial place of a wealthy patron, Dorinda Ashlin, who died in 1884 in Cork, so the oratory was never used, and lies empty to this day. Dorinda was the mother of the famous architect, George Ashlin, and she in fact lived with the nuns in the convent, and took her vows on her death bed. The cemetery is now full, and the nuns have a plot in Mount Venus, near Rathfarnham.

The 5-acre walled garden is still located to the north east of the old farmyard, and the hen runs and bull paddock were to the east of the old farmyard.

The walled garden is still a most attractive feature of the estate. The 4-metre high wall is brickfaced internally, and rubble granite faced externally, and there is a centre east-to-west dividing wall, resulting in two large gardens. Both gardens still contain orchards, and drills of vegetables. The long wrought iron framed glasshouse at the north end comprises a brick wall, against which the curved glass and frame rests. There are three compartments in the glass house, and a metal plate records the maker as W. and D. Bailey of 272, Holborn, London, probably in the early 19th century. Ogee shaped brick arches are a feature of the door and window at both ends of the glass house, and this architectural feature is carried through into the remains of a partly demolished Shell house, a residence, outside the north east corner of the walled garden. The nuns cemetery adjoins the south east corner of this garden. Older glass houses and a duck pond outside the south end of the walled garden have now disappeared.

The path adjoining the east side of the walled garden is known as Sacred Heart Alley, and is entered at the north end via a pair of lovely wrought iron gates, made by Richard Turner of Hammersmith Works, Ballsbridge, Dublin, the same firm who made the famous glass houses in the Botanic Gardens in Glasnevin, and who was also involved in Kew Gardens, London. These Turner gates possibly came from the Great Industrial Exhibition in 1853, which was financed by William Dargan. Another identical set of Turner gates grace the entrance to 201, Lower Kilmacud Road, a modest house (presently being extended), still occupied by the nuns, and one wonders if these were the original entrance gates opposite the front of the convent.

The nuns ran the farm as a business, employing a steward and various workmen. Excess produce was sold off, such as in 1883, when 47 cocks of hay were auctioned, or 1909, when 160 cocks were auctioned. The nuns exhibited the fruit of their orchard in various horticultural shows, such as the 1930 South County Dublin Show, when they achieved 1st place for two of their apples (Charles Ross, and Cox's Orange Pippin), and other prizes for their Allington Pippins, Russets, Peasgood Nonsuch, and Warners King, in addition to their beet, onions, and turnips.

In the past, the nuns hired out their workmen and machinery to other religious estates, such as the Christian Brothers in St. Helens (now a hotel), St. Raphaels Convent in Kilmacud, etc. Sometimes neighbours rented out spare fields to the Mount Anville nuns, where extra hay could be cut, e.g. Jennings field in Roebuck Hill, near the Foster Avenue junction. The nuns also had a special relationship with Blackrock College, allowing the Holy Ghost fathers to graze their cattle in Mount Anville farm, so that the priest's fields could be used for rugby.

Up until recent decades, the convent was better known as The Retreat House, where outsiders were allowed in for a few days of prayer and holy sermons. One retreat was reserved for the acting profession, where comedians such as Jimmy O'Dea and Maureen Potter took a few days off before Easter to reflect and pray in the main school chapel, whilst residing in the convent.

☺

Nowadays Mount Anville School is a sprawling complex of old buildings, including numerous ad hoc extensions, with the Secondary School in the west wing, the Junior School in the middle wing, and the Montessori School nearest the former convent. There is no imposing main entrance, but instead of variety of small doors provide access into the different sections. About 1,100 pupils are looked after by about 75 teachers.

The Montessori comprises low infants, high infants, 1st and 2nd years of Junior School, and caters for boys and girls. All these children have their separate colourful outdoor playing area beside the south end of the chapel.

The Junior School comprises the 3rd, 4th, 5th and 6th years of Primary education, and each year has two classes of mixed ability.

The Senior School provides six years of secondary education (including a 4th year Transition period after the Junior/Intermediate Cert exams), and there are four classes in each year, all of mixed ability, i.e. slow and fast learners all in the one class. Occasionally an additional fifth class might be required in any one year. Senior School has the largest number of pupils, since girls from the

Mount Anville Primary School (see later Chapter) and other schools are eligible for admission. Thus a child can enter at 2-3 years of age, and leave at 18 or 19 years of age, paying an average of about €5,000 per annum. It should be noted that the Government pays all the teacher's salaries, including the nuns, and the school fees only fund extra-curricular subjects. Despite this, the Government has little or no say in the running of the school. A nine member Board of Management runs the school, comprising four trustees (two nuns and two others), two parent representatives, two staff reps, and the school principal acts as secretary. Thus the parents and staff can never outvote the trustees/principal, who make all the important decisions.

One might wonder if school has become any easier for children, but believe it or not, even Leaving Cert adults of 18-19 years of age still carry heavy bags of books on their backs, weighing up to two stone, although admittedly many travel on the private school bus, or get lifts from their parents. A dozen or two 5th and 6th years drive their own cars to school.

The girls still carry on the traditions of a bygone age, by appointing 16 prefects from the Leaving Cert class to act as mentors to the first four years of the secondary school, and these prefects are recognizable by the blue sash which they wear from shoulder to hip. 6th Year girls wear black knee length socks, whereas all other girls wear white socks. Most of the 6th Years are in fact adults, capable of voting and marrying, and have the privilege of their own small Common Room, including kettle, toaster and microwave. Another tradition is activated around Halloween, when the Leaving Cert girls wear their normal clothes to school for one day, and enjoy a party at the expense of the fifth year girls. A new trend is the Pre-Debs party, organized by the Leaving Cert girls themselves. The girls still talk about the ghosts of former boarders. The shop and Post Office on the Lower Kilmacud Road, opposite the back gate of Mount Anville, is still an institution for the girls, especially the 6th Year girls who are allowed out during school hours to buy sweets, etc. The "Bishops Door" (referring to Cardinal Cullen) is still so named and used, leading into the original boarding school. The turquoise (blue/green) uniform is still recognized in public areas, but this of course is completely different from what the girls wear to nightclubs in their spare time. However, the tradition which takes pride of place is the annual Year Book, a top class colour production, to remind each girl of their time in the school.

The nuns pride themselves on their outdoor activities, such as netball, tennis, hockey, athletics, and even a small amount of cricket, still adhering to the motto "a healthy mind in a healthy body", although there is no swimming pool or modern gym.

Mount Anville has a special relationship with Blackrock College, whereby some Mount Anville girls help the boys with their concerts and dramas, although the arrangement does not work in reverse!

Nowadays, the nuns have disappeared from the teaching staff, which mostly comprises lay women, many of them married. The standard of education is the same as most Dublin schools, and quite a few girls take "private grinds" (extra tuition), to make up for some teacher's deficiencies. Up to about 10% of girls leave after 5th Year (sometimes after 4th Year) to complete their Leaving Cert course in the Institute of Education, Lower Leeson Street, which prepares them for the culture shock of Third Level Education.

In 1995, the nuns built a group of bungalows near the old farmyard, just south of the cemetery, called the Sophie Barat Homes, to cater for elderly former Mount Anville students who have fallen on hard times. There are 23 homes, spread over eight blocks, and a central communal building, with resident matron.

☺

The convent recently moved out of the late Georgian house, and the nuns now live in small groups of two to three, in 36 and 38, Mount Anville Park, 96, Mount Anville Wood, and 201, Lower Kilmacud Road. Many nuns are old and reside in Cedar House Nursing Home. The novitiate is long disused, and now is used as part of the Junior School.

The original convent doesn't appear to have changed much since Dargan's time in the middle of the 19th Century, being six bays wide and in depth, and two stories over basement. The front basement windows are barely visible from the forecourt, but the east basement windows, and one rear basement window, are not visible, since they are below a raised lawn, which in turn is surrounded by a charming cast iron ornate balustrade along the east side of the house, with especially decorative entrance gates. The external walls of the convent are smooth rendered, windows are vertical sliding timber sash pattern, and visible parts of the roof are pitched and slated, with a central copper flat area. The top floor of the tower contains a large cold water storage tank, but the decorative ceiling mouldings here remind us of its function as a good quality viewing room. Even the cast iron staircase balustrade in the tower is noteworthy. Inside the house, there is a large courtyard-style hall in the centre, two storeys high, lit by a large dome style roof light. The various rooms open off the inner hall, and a gallery on three sides at first floor level, with attractive cast iron balustrade, provides an attractive focal point, as does the matching staircase. Main ground floor rooms have mahogany paneled doors, carved architraves, ornate plaster cornices, and other plaster features, in addition to some lovely marble fireplaces. The three east rooms on the ground floor have sliding interconnecting doors, so that one very long room can be created for parties, etc.

The ashlar granite single storey gate lodge is very imposing, and appears to date from the 1840's. Originally there was a gate lodge almost opposite the house. Some of the old boundary walls can still be seen, especially on the Kilmacud side, and these are of light brown rubble granite, similar to the stone used in the original boarding school.

☺

To mark the 300th anniversary of Mount Merrion, the school intends putting the big mechanical clock from the original boarding school attic, and the three Sheridan bells, on permanent display in one of the school rooms.

1940's aerial. Note Knockrabo in rear right. (NL)

1960's aerial, with Deerpark in centre foreground. (Aerofilms)

Early 20th century postcard (SK)

Early 20th century postcard of walled garden and glasshouse/vinery. (SK)

2010 view

Joinery and plasterwork in Reception rooms.

81

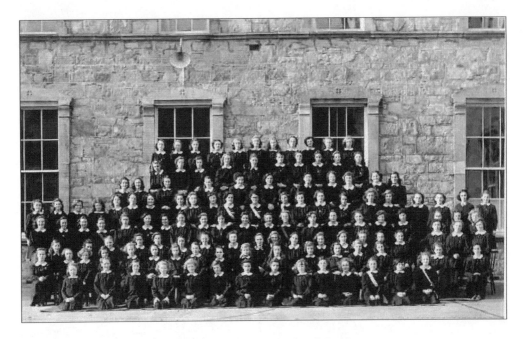

1949 Boarders in Junior School

1949 National School (photo taken in front of Boarding School).

Chapter 7

MOUNT ANVILLE PRIMARY SCHOOL

The Ladies of the Sacred Heart (this title was used for many decades to distinguish them from lay people) bought Mount Anville in 1865, and immediately began building a very large boarding school, much too large for their 30 girls, but intended for a future expansion in numbers. They also set up an "extern school" for poor children, although there were enough National Schools in Stillorgan and Kilmacud. A room in the single storey farmyard buildings was chosen for the school, but a large extension was built in 1870. The nuns obtained Board of Education approval in 1879, and thereafter the Government paid all of the school bills and salaries. The archives of the Board record the facilities in 1879, the school being single storey and slated, with three interlinked rooms (one unused), sized 49 ft x 24 ft x 10 ft high, 20 ft x 24 ft, and 19 ft x 24 ft. Two untrained nuns did the teaching 5 days a week, and 4½ hours each day, and the pupils paid 1d per week. 10 boys and 64 girls were present on the date of inspection, although there were 19 boys and 92 girls on the roll book (register).

The Board archives record an average attendance of 130 pupils in 1926, and this seems to have been the norm up until the mid 1950's. In 1926, there was one nun and two lay assistants, although Sr. Stewart ran into problems with the Board, since she was not qualified to teach Irish, so important after the founding of the Irish Free State.

One of the nuns who taught here in the late 1940's has fond memories of the school, but doesn't miss the smell of pigs from the adjoining farmyard. She recalls that two groups of pupils were taught by two different teachers in the one room, with half of the pupils facing one way, and the rest facing the other way. One class did vocal work, while the other did quiet work, and then reversed roles. Each group comprised different classes, e.g. 3rd and 4th Class would all be in the same group.

In 1955, the school moved to a new purpose-built premises on a 4 acre site, a few hundred metres further to the east along Lower Kilmacud Road, in a part of the nun's farm known as Botany Bay. This is a single storey slated building, with two long wings housing the classrooms, and a hall in the centre. The woodblock floors are still in the classrooms and the hall, and coloured terrazzo screeds in the corridors. The various corridor walls (and some ceilings) are beautifully decorated with colourful floral scenes, which add to the homely nature of the school. A playing yard is included, and a small vegetable/flower garden. The rear disused field will cater for future expansion. Pupil numbers increased to 402 in 1957, rising to 700 in the 1960's, but dropping down to 300 in 1990. After enlarging the original classrooms in 2009, the school nowadays caters for 415 girls, aged 4-13, looked after by 20 teachers and 2 special needs assistants. In the early years of the new school building, infant boys were catered for, but this stopped around 1999. Many of the girls go into the fee paying Senior School, after a free education in the primary school. The primary school uniform includes a tartan skirt, to distinguish the girls from the fee paying Junior School.

Part of the historic old farmyard and old national school is still in existence. The 1870 part of the school was demolished to pave the way for new houses in Mount Anville Lawn in the 1970's, but most of the original room from 1865 is still there and used as a store. The south side of the farmyard buildings is used by the family of one of the convent workmen, although the centre archway has been converted into a room, and an extra storey added in the 1950's. The old school gate is still visible, although blocked up, in the stone boundary wall, which now fronts No. 257, Lower Kilmacud Road. There is still a stone-lined well in the centre of the farmyard, including a horse trough, and this supplies water to the large greenhouses inside the walled garden.

1914 postcard (SK)

2006 remains of farmyard – single storey section was original school.

Early 20ᵗʰ century postcard of farmyard. (SK)

2006 view of new school on Kilmacud Rd.

Chapter 8

MOUNT ANVILLE PERIOD HOUSES

Knockrabo

This seven bay, two storey over basement late Georgian mansion, on 22 acres, was better known as Mount Anville House (although sometimes called Mount Anville Park!), and its most famous owner was Christopher Palles, who was Lord Chief Baron of the Court of Exchequer (nowadays would be called the President of the High Court) from 1874 – 1916. He bought Mount Anville House in 1885, and died there in 1920. He was known as a devout Catholic, and even had an oratory in the house, although he frequented the nun's chapel across the road in Mount Anville Convent.

The external style of the house was in fact similar to the convent, except that the former had a feature verandah at ground floor level for the full length of the rear elevation and the end elevations. There was also a viewing tower in the centre of the roof, similar to the nun's belvedere. Palles also had a townhouse at No. 28, Fitzwilliam Place, at the corner of Lower Leeson Street, which he bought in 1879, and he added a small chapel to the rear, designed by George Ashlin. The same architect has associations with Mount Anville boarding school.

The 1901 Census lists 69-year old Palles as the occupier of Knockrabo, accompanied by his 37-year old son, one boarder, one visitor, a housekeeper, a cook, two housemaids, a kitchen maid, a scullery maid, a butler, two footmen, a stable helper, an under-gardener, and a private soldier (presumably for security purposes).

Henry Roe (whiskey fame) was the occupier of the house before Palles, and the lessor was Orme, related to the Westby family in nearby Roebuck Castle.

The Sacred Heart nuns must have been very disappointed when a Protestant Secondary Boarding School, PNEU, acquired the property in 1942. The Parents National Education Union was founded in Chichester (England) by Charlotte Mason (1842 – 1923), an educationalist. The Irish Principal was Mrs J. H. Waller, and the school catered for female boarders, in addition to a Day school for young boys and girls. The girls wore a light blue uniform, and attended religious services in nearby Taney Church. The house name was changed to Knockrabo (Cnoc or hill of Roebuck), in order to avoid confusion with Mount Anville Convent across the road. The school lasted until 1957, when it was sold to the Dublin Gas Company Sports Club. The club had a pitch and putt course, a bowling green, tennis courts, and football pitches, and the maintenance staff were provided with apartments in the old house and the two gate lodges. The Ski Club of Ireland was founded in 1963, and for a few years, took a subletting of part of the Gas Company grounds, and ran its first slope here. They moved to Kilternan when Knockrabo was sold to Bank of Ireland. The Gas Company sold the property to the Bank of Ireland Sports Club in the mid 1970's, and the bank demolished the old house and outbuildings, to make way for more outdoor activities. The bank acquired the adjoining smaller Georgian house, Cedarmount (once called Mount Anville Cottage), in 1988, and this house is still standing, although the new timber-clad rear extension might not appeal to everyone. The combined property of 24 acres was sold in 1999. and awaits redevelopment. **(Photo on p.79)**

Roebuck Hill

The study of maps and street directories for the 19th century can be very confusing, because similar names were often used for different houses in the same locality, and sometimes new owners abandoned the old name in favour of some other name. Roebuck is especially confusing, and to a lesser extent, so is Mount Anville.

Roebuck Hill (once called The Paddock) is an early 19th century two storey three bay house, with a single storey wing at each end, facing north, at the corner of Mount Anville Road and Roebuck Road. Its five bay side elevation is probably better known to the upper-deck travellers on Dublin Bus, as is the lovely side flower garden. The land around here was leased in 1808 by William Conyngham Plunkett to John Walsh, for the lives of Henry, William, and James Kemmis, and there was a covenant to build within five years a good and substantial dwelling house, and expend thereon at least £500 – this presumably refers to the building of Roebuck Hill. The side wings are probably additions, and likewise, a variety of rear extensions. The property passed to Walsh's daughter, Elizabeth Scully, but by 1864, the Landed Estates Court sold the house and other adjoining properties up as far as Beverston, to George Kinahan (who rented Roebuck Hill) for £2,210.

The Orme family lived here in the mid 20th century, and were related to the Westby family of nearby Roebuck Castle. When builder, Joe Jennings, bought this house and six acres from Miss Orme in 1961, James Adam, auctioneers, described the accommodation: "double drawingroom with conservatory, diningroom, breakfastroom, cloakroom, six bedrooms, dressingroom, kitchen, maid's rooms, annex containing four rooms, also a pavilion, formerly a billiards room, enclosed stable yard and out-offices, walled-in garden, vegetable garden". The Jennings later built a block of flats to the south, Moytura, and more recently built a modern development of apartments to the north of the house. The latter site was a small field for many years, inhabited only by Tom the donkey, so much loved by countless Mount Anville schoolgirls. Jennings also built the Knocknashee housing estate.

Roebuck Hill, 2006

Roebuck Hall

This imposing Victorian two storey over basement house, is hidden away in the midst of a 1960's housing estate, known as The Palms. The house was converted into about 18 flats in 1993, but still features extensive granite dressings on the front elevation.

Ardilea House (formerly Roebuck Cottage)

Going uphill past Roebuck Hill, a curved granite boundary wall and gates, together with an attractive granite gate lodge, gives the impression of entering an important house. Market gardener, Frank Walker, bought the farm in 1946, and also kept a herd of Jersey cows. The house was burnt to the ground in March, 1959, but Frank and his wife, and two daughters, escaped injury. A Limerick builder, O'Callaghan, acquired the farm, and in the early 1960's built an estate of large bungalows, naming each road after a famous university, such as Louvain, Sorbonne, Salamanca etc. He also built a large bungalow for himself, on five acres, which was sold in 1977 to the legendary Joe Walsh, from Bangor in County Down (who founded Joe Walsh Tours in 1961). Another famous Dublin builder, Joe Cosgrave, bought the bungalow in 1997, as his residence, and in 2000 built ten very exclusive houses (Ardilea Wood) on part of the five acres, while still retaining his bungalow and large garden.

The next house going uphill past Ardilea House was **Shanavaun** (previously called Wellfield and then Janeville Cottage), but this was demolished in the late 1970's, to make way for an estate of detached houses, called Ardilea Downs, selling in 1980 for £85,000 each.

Next in line was **Margretta** (previously called Roebuck Mount, and Mount Anville), which is now the site of a Council Depot/yard, for the Roads Department, and maintenance equipment for nearby Deerpark.

Beverston, dating from around 1852, is still standing to the west of the Council depot, but now surrounded by a few modern detached houses.

Travelling towards Goatstown crossroads, the last period property is **Hollywood House**, on two acres, a three bay, two storey over basement, early Victorian house, with its rear elevations facing the public road. The north section is the original, and then various south extensions added in the early years. The three reception rooms on the ground floor are exceptionally spacious, with the two in the west wing having double dividing doors between them, and there are nice cornices and joinery throughout the ground and first floors. Its old stables have been converted and extended into two detached two-storey houses, and an extra house built, all called 1,2,3 Hollywood Mews.

Hollywood House in 1987   Lodge for Ardilea House

Sandwiched between Hollywood House and Cedarmount House, is a collection of smallish old houses, mostly late Georgian, the main one being **Mount Anville Lodge**, backing directly onto Mount Anville Road. This was subdivided to form Thendara (also called Bloomsbury) and The Garth, although the breakfastroom in the former is now under a bedroom in the latter! "Chimes" is a 1960's detached house between Thendara and Hollywood Mews, built in the original walled garden of Hollywood House.

Around 200 acres of land around here was originally leased for 400 years from 1799, by Lord Trimleston to Thomas Kemmis, and he in turn sub-let smaller parcels, including Mount Anville Convent, Roebuck Hill, and Knockrabo etc. The Kemmis family (Church of Ireland) hailed from County Laois, and had some "men of cloth" in the family. Thomas was Crown Solicitor, and acquired a lot of land in various counties. He married Anne White, and this name is still familiar in the Mount Anville locality. There are family burial plots in Mount Jerome (Harolds Cross) and Portlaoise (previously called Maryborough, because it was "settled" by Queen Mary).

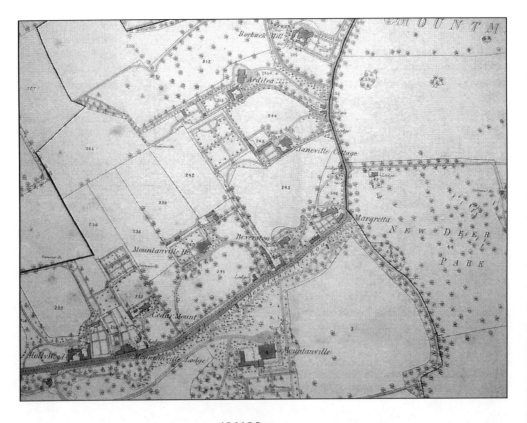

1866 Map. (NA1)

90

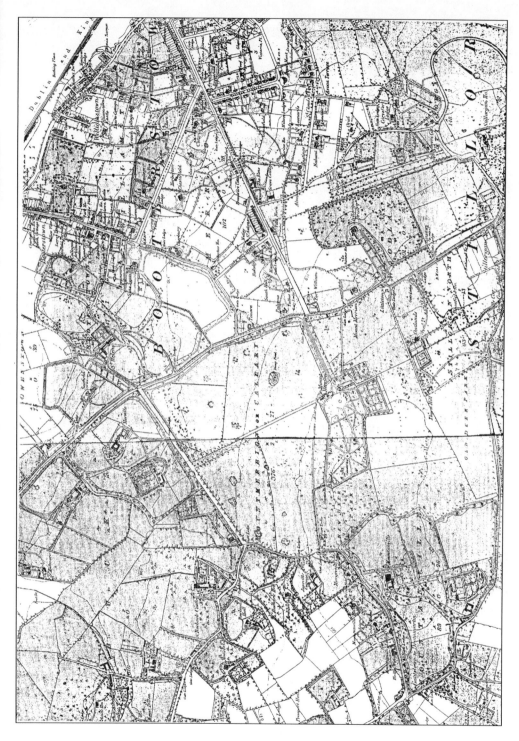

Ordnance Survey Map: 1869. (TC)

Chapter 9

THORNHILL - OATLANDS - BEAUFIELD

Thornhill House

This late-18th century house is situated on part of the former estate of the Earl of Carysfort, being part of a much larger parcel of land, which included Thornhill, Oatlands, Beaufield, and most of the village of Stillorgan, all let by Thomas Addis Emmet to William Fleming for 95 years from 1799. In 1880, the Landed Estates Court sold this entire parcel of land, which was at that stage owned by Richard Guinness Hill (deceased), and the Particulars make very interesting reading. The parcel was described as "all that part of Stillorgan, in the County of Dublin, formerly held by Robert Emmet, but now in the possession of said Thomas Addis Emmet or his under tenants, comprising by estimate 44 acres, 3 roods and 27 perches, etc." (63 acres, 3 roods, and 13 perches in Statute measure). Part of the annual rent included "one fat hog" every Christmas. Robert Emmet was the Protestant patriot executed in 1803, at the age of 25, after his unsuccessful uprising in Dublin.

Thornhill (Lot 3 on map) comprised 16 acres, and had a gate lodge at the south west corner, off the present Kilmacud Road. The occupiers also had a right of way along Callary Lane through the north side of Oatlands, leading to the Stillorgan Road, at which there was another gate lodge beside Littleton. Viscount Fitzwilliam also had a right of way from his adjoining demesne through Callary Lane, across Thornhill and Oatlands.

Oatlands (Lot 4) comprised 13 acres. Littleton was a small plot/house beside the east end of Callary Lane (the lane is still here, but overgrown).

Beaufield (Lot 6) was 25 acres, and included Garnaville Cottage and Ornee Cottage along Kilmacud Road.

Stillorgan village (Lot 7) comprised 18 acres, with a frontage to Stillorgan Road and Kilmacud Road, and included the cottages now known as The Hill. The Joly family leased various small pieces of land. The inhabitants of Stillorgan were entitled to draw water from the well at the south east corner of the present shopping centre.

James Forrest, a 78-year old silk merchant, occupied Thornhill at the time of the 1901 Census, and describes the house as having 5 front windows, and 13 rooms. There was a stable, a coachhouse, a harness room, a cowhouse, a calf house, a piggery, 3 fowl houses, two turf houses and a laundry.

Within a few years of the census, the property must have reverted to the landlord, since the Earl of Carysfort (of Glenart, Co. Wicklow) let it again for 50 years from 1908 to Thomas Talbot Power of Inverusk, Ballybrack, Co. Dublin, and comprising 16 acres, 22 perches, including gate lodges, at an annual rent of £125. The Power family were famous whiskey distillers based in Thomas Street (Johns Lane), from 1791, and were the first company to sell their whiskey in miniature bottles called "Baby Powers". The Powers were from Wexford, and married into the Talbot family, also from Wexford. Sir Thomas Talbot Power died in 1930. In due course, the Ryan family became the leaders of the distillery. The company merged in 1966 with rivals, John Jameson and Son, and Cork Distillers Company, to form Irish Distillers. Bushmills in Northern Ireland joined the group in 1972. A new central distillery was built in Middleton, Cork, in 1975, and the various constituent plants closed. Since 1988, Irish Distillers became part of Pernod-Ricard. The old John's Lane distillery in Thomas Street is now the National College of Art and Design.

Thornhill

93

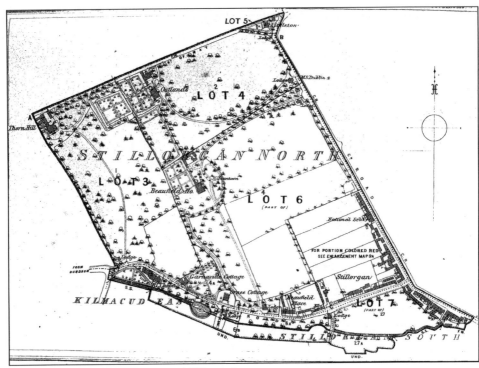

1880 estate map. (NA1)

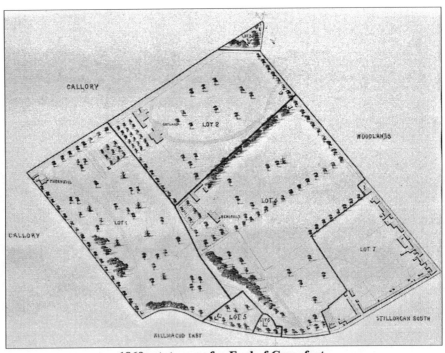

1860 estate map for Earl of Carysfort.
Plot numbers are different from the 1880 map above. (NA1)

94

Prior to acquiring Thornhill, Thomas Talbot Power rented for a few years the adjoining Mount Merrion House from the Pembroke/Fitzwilliam estate, and the 1901 Census records the 37 year old Thomas living here with his 39-year old Australian born wife, Margaret (both Catholics). His wife, in fact, was a daughter of Charles Owen Martin from nearby Beaufield House. The family firm of T & C Martin, were famous in Dublin as timber merchants and builders providers, although are more often described as being the employers of Matt Talbot. Thomas and Margaret had married young, he at age 20 and she 22. Their staff in Mount Merrion House included a lady's maid, a kitchen maid, a house maid, a cook, a butler and a coachman.

The 1911 Census records the Talbot Powers still in Thornhill, comprising a chauffeur, a cook, a parlour maid, a house maid and lady's maid.

In the 1930's, William Ryan, a nephew of Sir Thomas Talbot Power, and co-director of John Power and Son Ltd, acquired Thornhill. One of his sons, Clem Ryan, still fondly remembers his childhood in the house, including open fields all around, some with wheat growing, their hens and pigs, and their Jersey cows. He also remembers the "mass path" from their house to the nearby Mount Merrion House (by then a Catholic chapel), and also the deer which were kept there on behalf of the Ward Union Hunt (North County Dublin).

Following the death of Philomena Ryan in 1959, the Ryan family sold a large part of Thornhill to P.V. Doyle, a builder (and later hotelier), who immediately built the Cherrygarth estate of 60 houses, some two storey, but mostly bungalows. The original lodge on Kilmacud Road was demolished by the County Council in the 1970's, to allow road widening, and a new bungalow built further back from the road.

The old house is still occupied by P.V. Doyle's widow, Margaret Doyle (nee Mulvey), and has a lovely garden extending to three acres. In fact, most of the old stone high boundary walls are still in position. The front of the house is three bays wide, and two storey over basement, although the latter is hidden by a ramped flower bed. However, the house is much deeper, resulting from various extensions to the rear over the years.

The Childrens House

Some might think of a doll's house or a tree house, but this in fact is a charming Montessori school, barely visible, opposite the old Kilmacud chapel-of-ease, catering for children in the 3-12 age bracket, sharing an entrance with Homefield, a private bungalow.

The Montessori method of teaching young children was developed in Rome when Dr. Maria Montessori, a physician, opened her first school, Casa dei Bambini (Children's House) in 1907. Young children learn by touching, seeing and hearing, instead of the "parrot" system (constant repetition) used in most national schools. In the Montessori method, the infant is taught to break down a word into much smaller parts, and to speak or mouth the individual letters slowly, phonetically, so as to eventually merge into the word, e.g. d-o-g. In other words, the ear plays a bigger part than the eye. Similar concepts are used to teach children basic life skills, the overriding principle being that a child is essentially capable of teaching themselves with the correct guidance.

The Children's House

In 1925, the first official Montessori school opened in the Ursaline Convent, Waterford, followed in 1928 by a Children's House in the Junior School of the Dominican Convent, Sion Hill, Mount Merrion Avenue, the latter developing into the country's first 6-month Montessori Teacher Training Course (1933-1934).

Veronica Ryan was born in 1921, in "Ellerslie", Temple Road, Rathmines, to William Ryan and Philomena Smith-Steinmetz. Veronica trained in the Montessori method in Sion Hill, and taught in the Sacred Heart Convent in Monkstown from 1947 – 1949. In 1950, she started her own school in one room of the family's new home, Thornhill House, with 6 youngsters. Her parents paid for a purpose-built Montessori school on a half acre wooded site at the south-east corner of their estate, the first such school in Ireland, containing two large classrooms, teacher's room, and toilets, with secure and colourful external play areas. The school opened on 13th October 1952, with Veronica in charge of 35 children, aged 3-6, and soon afterwards was joined by Beppa Sharkey, who looked after 35 children aged 6-9. The school flourished, and is still going strong to this day, having been extended in 2010. The school now has 70 pupils, in the 3-12 age bracket, and 7 teachers, all run by Ms Micaela Kuh, who took over about five years ago, when Madeline Coen retired. The school receives no government funding whatsoever, is non-denominational, and is run as a non-profit organization by a voluntary Board.

Veronica built a large bungalow for herself in the mid 1950's, on the adjoining 1.8 acre site (part of her parents property), calling it Homefield. Shortly after her mother, Philomena, died in 1959, the old house, Thornhill, was sold to builder, P.V. Doyle, who went on to build Cherrygarth, an estate of bungalows and some two storey houses, but Veronica retained the school and Homefield.

Sadly, Veronica died in 1966, aged only 45, and her brother John Ryan acquired the bungalow. When John's second wife, Bunty, died in 1991, he sold the property. Homefield enjoys the benefit of a rear vehicular tradesman's entrance from Cherrygarth estate, so redevelopment of this quite corner of the locality may not be too far off, or maybe the Children's House will expand to become a Children's Hamlet.

Oatlands

The old Oatlands House and 13 acres was part of a larger estate, leased by the Emmet family from 1799, but when the Landed Estates Court sold the entire estate in 1880, the owner was Richard Guinness Hill, and Oatlands was leased to Thomas Fry for 85 years from 1808, at a rent of £92 6s 2d per annum. The house was obviously sublet, since Matthew Pollock occupied it from 1840 – 1910, and he in fact bought it from the Landed Estate Court in 1880. Later occupiers included solicitor Fred Darley from 1910 – 1916, Sir John Ross, Lord Chancellor, from 1916 – 1926, and Peter O'Connell from 1926 – 1951. Pollock is probably the most famous occupier, being a partner in the wholesale drapers, Ferrier Pollock, who owned Powerscourt House in South William Street, from 1835 – 1981, when it was sold and converted into a chic shopping centre.

Oatlands was two storey over basement, five bays wide, and had an observatory/telescope on the roof, attributed to Sir Howard Grubb.

The Christian Brothers bought the property in 1951 as a home for themselves, and a fee-paying secondary school, seeing Mount Merrion as an affluent locality, bearing in mind that secondary education was not the norm in that era. The school opened that same year with 14 boys in first year, and 4 boys in second year.

By 1953, a new two storey school was opened alongside the old house, and this operated as both a primary and secondary school, until a separate secondary school was opened beside the Stillorgan Road in 1955. The builder, Geraghty, presented the Brothers with an engraved silver key.

Oatlands before demolition. (CBS)

With the advent of free secondary education in 1967, the Brothers were reluctant to join the scheme initially, because they feared the loss of £39 per annum, and were worried about a general lowering of standards in the country. However, common sense prevailed, and they had to build a single storey prefab extension in 1969, to cater for the extra students, with an extra storey on stilts on top of that 30-years later. A basic detached sports hall was provided in 1980, to complement sports played in the large field between the primary and secondary schools. In 2010 the prefabs under the stilts were replaced by permanent construction, and new prefabs provided in the rear yard. The large carpark now has more student cars than teachers cars.

September 2005 was a milestone, when girls were admitted for the first time to the primary school, but they cannot proceed into the secondary school.

There are no brothers teaching there now, but they still own and control the schools. The Secondary school has 500 pupils, 45 teachers, and 4 special needs assistants. The Primary School has 320 pupils, 19 teachers, and 5 special needs assistants.

When free secondary education was introduced in 1967, the Brothers expected a boom time, and so built themselves a new modern monastery beside the old house. The architect, Ronnie Tallon, designed a flat roofed box building, with a small internal courtyard, all enclosed by glass. The house catered for 28 brothers and 2 maids, cost £106,000, and was opened in 1968. Later that year, the old mansion house was demolished.

Primary school at rear left, monastery at rear right, and college at front.
Littleton in right front corner. (CBS)

The Christian Brothers in Ireland are now almost extinct, and in 2008 they transferred their schools to a private trust, on strict condition that the Catholic ethos is maintained. The Dept. of Education has funded these schools for many decades by paying the salaries of the teachers, and grant-aiding buildings and extensions (with financial assistance from the local community). The Brothers will obviously keep on, or sell, the monastery, since they have a separate entrance off the Stillorgan Road, via the overgrown and abandoned Callary Lane. Incidentally, the quaint lodge at the east end of the lane was attached to the original Thornhill House as a second entrance, but is now privately owned, and in recent years was extensively extended.

Monastery

Oatlands College/Secondary School

Littleton

Between Oatlands College and the bottom of Trees Road, is a compact late Georgian villa. Originally the hall door was in the centre of the first floor, approached by an external flight of stone steps, but this arrangement no longer exists. The cast iron gates and granite pillars are a noteworthy feature. The road outside is now a cul-de-sac, but this was originally the only road through Stillorgan. Torbett was a previous occupier.

Beaufield

Nowadays, Beaufield Mews is famous as an "olde worlde" restaurant cum antiques shop/art gallery, because of the good food and superb rear garden, but part of the attraction lies in the patchwork of old buildings, which in fact were the coachhouse/stables for the main mansion house, Beaufield.

The 25-acre Beaufield estate was originally part of a larger estate, under an old 1799 Robert Emmet lease, and extended down to the present Kilmacud Road, but did not include the main village of Stillorgan (the present shopping centre area), which was held by others under a separate lease. The properties on the Kilmacud Road included Garnaville Cottage and Ornee Cottage, and some smaller cottages called Beaufield Place, in the vicinity of the present Stillorgan Décor.

The early-Victorian house was similar in design to the nearby Oatlands, except smaller (three bays wide). Different families rented/owned it over its life, including Henry Darley, Patrick Sweetman, Martin, Comyn, etc. In fact, Thomas Shannon Martin bought the house in 1881 from the Landed Estates Court. In 1936, the County Council acquired, by Compulsory Purchase, a plot of 8 acres alongside Kilmacud Road, where they built a spacious estate of 68 workers two-storey cottages, Beaufield Park.

The Kirwan family acquired the remainder of the estate, including the main house and stables, from the Wilsons, in 1938, and sub-divided the house into flats/apartments. Valentine Kirwan was a solicitor, and he sold off parts of the estate to developers in the 1940/50's, who built the houses in Woodlands Avenue, etc. Then his wife, Doreen, converted the stables into an antique shop in 1948, plus a coffee shop in 1950, and expanded the coffee shop into a restaurant about ten years later.

Following a fire in 1987, the Kirwans sold the main house to a developer, who demolished the house, and built 33 townhouses and bungalows, called Beaufield Manor. Doreen's granddaughter, Julie Cox, now runs the restaurant, while Doreen's daughter, Jill Cox, runs the first floor antiques shop. Jill still maintains the wonderful garden, which is colourful all year around, but especially in August, when the flowers rival the Chelsea Flower Show. The head waiter, Paddy Rice, is still as efficient and good humoured as ever, after more than 43-years service, whose motto is: "Do it nice, or do it twice!" The entire complex of building, including the restaurant, is an ever changing art gallery, where living artists display their creativity, usually at reasonable prices. The restaurant was modernised in 2007, in the hope of attracting a more affluent younger clientele, while still pleasing the regular older set, especially the family groups who have enjoyed Sunday lunch for the last 20 years.

Beaufield Mews in 2006

Beaufield Mews Garden

Jill Cox, Paddy Rice, Julie Cox.
(2010 photo by Jill Cox)

Chapter 10

UCD – ROEBUCK - HERMITAGE

Trinity College, founded in 1592, was originally the only university in Dublin, but not open to Catholics, until about 200 years later, when Catholics were admitted to study, but not to lecture or manage. At the request of the Irish hierarchy, Father John Henry Newman opened the Catholic University in 1854, at 86, St. Stephens Green, a small townhouse. Newman was an Englishman, and a Protestant, but converted to Catholicism in 1845, at the age of 44. He was ordained a priest in England only in 1847. As the first Rector of the Catholic University in Dublin, he appointed a lot of his friends from England as lecturers, but he resigned in 1859, and returned to England. However, he should be credited with the beautiful adjoining University Church, which opened in 1856. In the 1880's, other colleges became constituent colleges of the Catholic University, including Blackrock College, Clonliffe College, Terenure College, Maynooth College.

Outside Dublin, an Act of 1845 created the Queens Colleges of Cork, Galway, and Belfast, but these colleges were not acceptable to the Catholic church.

The Government set up the Royal University of Ireland in 1882, comprising the colleges of Cork, Galway, Belfast, in addition to a college in Earlsfort Terrace, located in the former Great Exhibition buildings. By 1908, the Irish Universities Act had been introduced, creating the National University of Ireland, with its constituent colleges of UCD, UCG and UCC, all now acceptable to the Catholic church. UCD adopted Earlsfort Terrace as their new home, although there were some faculties elsewhere, such as the College of Science in the present Government Buildings. In 1914, a new university was built on the site of the Royal University in Earlsfort Terrace.

In 1933, UCD bought Belfield House in Donnybrook, with 44 acres, for £8,000, for use as their sports grounds, at which stage, there were already five grass tennis courts and a walled garden. Belfield was built in 1801 for the La Touche family, famous bankers. The small walled sunken garden is a little gem, and is still there containing lovely roses and low box hedges. The house has recently been restored to its former glory, and is now the Clinton Institute for American Studies.

By 1946, 12 acres at Roebuck Castle was leased from the Little Sisters of the Poor, as additional sports grounds. Over the next 15 years, other houses with land were bought, such as Ardmore, Montrose, Thornfield, and Merville with 60-acres in 1951-1953.

By 1960, the Government had approved the plan to move UCD from Earlsfort Terrace to Belfield (as the various houses and lands were collectively called), and by autumn 1964, the new science building was opened. By 1970, the arts block was completed, followed by the library in 1973. Succeeding decades saw the purchase of more land, and new buildings are still being erected to the present day. Even recently, the former Phillips factory on Roebuck Road was acquired, and the college can now boast of 142 hectares (350 acres).

Religious rivalries between Trinity College and UCD were re-ignited in 1944, when Archbishop McQuaid issued an order from church pulpits, prohibiting all Catholics from sending their children to Trinity, on pain of a mortal sin, and eternal damnation in hell, unless he granted special permission. However, by June 1970, McQuaid was forced to cancel his dictate. Even prior to the McQuaid era, the Catholic Church discouraged the laity from attending Trinity, but there was always a sizeable minority in that college.

The initial concept for Belfield was a noble one, but it seems that the governing body never had a proper long term vision or masterplan. Hence the campus is now a sprawling mess, and the core buildings typify the "concrete jungle". Poor architecture in general abounds, especially the library, with its external concrete shades, and even the recent residential blocks, with their use of bare concrete blockwork, bear a strong resemblance to army barracks. The faculty of architecture is on the periphery of the campus, occupying an old Masonic Boys School. Because Architecture has its own library, etc., it is almost self contained, and does not properly engage in cross pollenisation of ideas and experiences with students in other faculties. Likewise, the faculty of Law occupies the old Roebuck Castle at the south-west periphery of the campus. The Vet faculty only moved from Ballsbridge a few years ago, to a new building on the north side of the campus. Up to March 2008, some engineering lectures were held in Earlsfort Terrace, beside the National Concert Hall. However, despite its wealth, and ongoing acquisition of more land, the College has not built an exam hall, resulting in the ridiculous situation, whereby, three times a year, thousands of students trek miles away to a large hall in the RDS, Ballsbridge.

The present campus population is around 22,000 students (17,000 undergraduates and 5,000 studying for masters and doctorates), and no doubt, some day they will be split into two colleges, one for Dublin City and the other for Dun Laoire Rathdown.

Not many people realise that Belfield campus is open to the public, and wonderful walks can be enjoyed, especially in the woods alongside Fosters Avenue and Roebuck Road. Here and there you will see the remains of former walled gardens from previous large houses, and occasionally a glimpse of a small stream. A little known gem is the former Magnetic Observatory near the country lane which leads from the pedestrian gate opposite Harlech Grove on Roebuck Road. This was built in Trinity College in 1838, and used by Humphrey Lloyd, to conduct "magnetic field" experiments, but was carefully demolished and rebuilt in Belfield in the early 1970's, to make way for the new Arts block in Trinity. However, UCD then allowed it to deteriorate into nearly a ruin, until it was restored in 2004, at considerable expense, and is now used as a 40-seat cinema, with state of the art equipment. The building looks like a Roman temple from the outside, complete with Portland stone cladding. UCD have named the building as the O'Kane Centre for Film Studies, in honour of their benefactor, Frank O'Kane, the co-founder of Mercury Engineering.

The large number of football pitches, a running track, and a large sports building (but no swimming pool) might lead you to think that you were in a sports academy, instead of a centre for third level education.

A few of the old houses survive, such as, Roebuck Castle, Belfield, Ardmore, and Merville.

Merville House

This mid 18th century house is built on part of the original Fitzwilliam estate, in the old townland of Owenstown. When Jonathan Barker surveyed the townland is 1762, his map showed the seat of Anthony Foster, including a sketch of the front elevation of the house, with its two bay windows, and a large walled garden some distance to the west of the main house (including its own small house). The estate included a quarry and a lime kiln, in addition to 3 cottages alongside Fosters Avenue. In later years, Foster became Chief Baron of the Irish Exchequer (a judge), and the road through the townland became known as Fosters Avenue. He was also a founder member of the (Royal) Dublin Society.

By the time of the Tithe Applotment Survey in the 1820's, William Downes, the Lord Chief Justice, was in occupation of Merville House. In 1830, it was recorded that Downes was the lessor, but had sublet to Michael Sweetman, and the 49 acre estate included farm buildings, in addition to a School House. Lieutenant General Henry Hall occupied for many decades in the 19th Century. The last most important occupant in the first half of the 20th Century was the Hume-Dudgeon family, who in later years, operated a riding school in the field alongside the Stillorgan Road. The Census of 1901 gives some useful information on the Dudgeon family, and their house. Joseph, aged 46, was a stockbroker, born in County Dublin. His wife, Isabella Best, was 39, and born in England. Their daughters Mary and Eileen were 13 and 11 respectively, while their son Joseph was 8. They had two visitors from overseas, and eight servants – a cook, two parlour maids, two laundry maids, a house maid, a kitchen maid, one nursery maid, and all 18 occupants were Protestants. They stated that the house had 30 rooms, and 20 front windows, plus 10 outbuildings.

Merville in 2006 (east side).

West side of Merville in mid 20th century. (UCD)

In the Census of 1911, there were 30 rooms, 42 front windows, and 17 outhouses, and Mary was absent. The 10 servants now comprised a cook, scullery maid, kitchen maid, two upper house maids, two parlour maids, a ladies maid, and two laundry maids. Other staff probably lived in separate cottages on the estate.

UCD bought the house and 60-acres in 1953 for £100,000, as part of a land bank for a future campus. After refurbishment, all research work in Biochemistry was moved to Merville, from the North Block, Earlsfort Terrace. The college again refurbished and extended the house in 2003, including the two original wings and courtyards, and it is now occupied by Nova UCD, a research facility. Internally, all the fireplaces are gone, but there are still some delicate plaster cornices and centrepieces, and some lovely moulded door architraves, in addition to a curved panelled door between the east and west hall. On the front elevation, a noteworthy feature is the cantilevered sandstone balcony, with cast iron balustrade, running the full width of the house. Until recently, the original walled garden was called Belfield Park, and was used jointly with the Football Association of Ireland as a soccer stadium. Now a brand-new building occupies the site, used by the National Institute for Bioprocessing, Research and Training. Two original rubble granite walls survive from the walled garden, and a brick wall.

Roebuck Castle

Ball records that Baron Trimleston, an officer in the Confederate Army, occupied Roebuck Castle, but that it was destroyed in the 1641 Rebellion.

The Downs Survey of the 1650's reported that there was a castle in Roebuck "in repair", and that Baron Trimleston, Irish Papist, was the owner, including 500 acres. The family name of Barnewall is probably more familiar, and was famous in legal circles for many generations.

Lewis, writing in 1837, reminds us that in 1534, Lord Trimleston, Lord Chancellor of Ireland, was in occupation, but in the 1680's, James II and the Duke of Berwick encamped here with their army. In 1783, Mr Tower was in occupation of the Castle and 104 acres, as shown on Lord Trimleston's map.

Around 1790, Lord Trimleston repaired the castle, and hence it looks very majestic in the picture painted in 1795, and included in Ball's History of County Dublin.

James Crofton acquired the property around 1800, and practically demolished and rebuilt the castle. Crofton Road in Dun Laoire commemorates the man, since he was one of the original Commissioners appointed to organise the construction of the new Harbour (c. 1818). By the 1860's, the Westby family were owners, and by 1870, they had carried out extensive alterations and improvements, including rebuilding the out-offices around the courtyard.

Roebuck Castle in 1765, by Gabriel Beranger. (NL)

1795 view of Castle. (GL)

Roebuck Castle and 72 acres was bought by the Little Sisters of the Poor in 1943, for £16,100. The names on the deeds are Elizabeth Downes, Helena

Smith, Teresa Lee (all of St. Patrick's, Kilmainham – their main house), Hanoria Boland and Mary Bridget Power (both of Hermitage – next door to Roebuck), and Catherine Neville, Loreto Holt, Mary Harney (all from Cork). The castle contained 6 bedrooms, diningroom, drawingroom, ante-room, 3 sittingrooms, 5 maids rooms, servants hall, 2 bathrooms, kitchen, scullery, and pantry. There was stabling for 16 horses, and tyings for 20 cows, in addition to a walled garden, with glasshouses. Two cottages, and a gate lodge, were included. Alongside the old castle, the nuns built a Nursing Home, including a separate church, to cater for about 100 elderly residents. The nuns were self-sufficient with their farming activities, including sheep and cows.

In 1946, the nuns sold UCD (of Earlsfort Terrace) a leasehold interest in 12 acres for £900, for use as a sports ground. Twenty years later, they sold the freehold interest in the sports ground to UCD for £10,000, including an extra 4 acres (in order to remove the restrictive covenant against building from the leasehold interest). UCD acquired another 13.4 acres in 1971, for £87,500, and a further 11 acres in 1985 for £800,000. Finally in 1986, the nuns sold UCD the Castle itself and 10 acres for £750,000. Most of the 50 acres acquired by UCD from the nuns is now occupied by the Belgrove Apartments and the Arts Block Extension. The beautiful two storey stone gate lodge on Roebuck Road, built in 1872, was sold off separately, around the same time, and nicely extended in recent years, and still bears the Westby coat of arms.

Next, the nuns sought Planning Permission for a private housing estate on the rest of their land (including a small part of the adjoining Hermitage), and after an oral hearing, An Bord Pleanala granted permission. Then 31.45 acres was sold in 1983 to Dwyer Nolan, who went on to build around 200 small townhouses on the estate (now called Roebuck Castle).

Initially UCD established the Michael Smurfit Graduate School of Business in Roebuck Castle, and also converted the more modern previous nursing home into student residences. The business school moved to the former Carysfort Training College in 1991, and now the Faculty of Law occupies the castle, and has converted the former church into a large ramped lecture theatre.

Most of the present exterior of Roebuck Castle is rendered, but there are large amounts of sandstone dressings around windows, and the west bay window is completely clad with sandstone. The three-bay arcade under this bay window is unusual, and may have been part of the original structural buttresses of the castle. Internally, many of the rooms, especially at first floor level, have attractive plaster cornices and marble fireplaces, and some rooms are embellished with slender green and red marble columns. The pine staircase

109

balustrade is noteworthy, as is the ramped hooded fireplace in the small entrance hall.

1866 map. (NA1)

Former Gate Lodge now extended.

Present Roebuck Castle, including fireplace in hall (as seen from stairs).

Little Sisters of the Poor/Hermitage.

These French nuns were founded in 1840 by Jeanne Jugan (recently made a Saint), to cater for elderly poor, and came to Waterford in 1871, and Kilmainham, Dublin in 1881. By 1943, the nuns decided to build another house for the poor aged, and acquired Roebuck Castle and a large farm. The previous year, the adjoining Hermitage House in Roebuck Road was also for sale by Frances Mansergh, also known in the operatic world as Fanny Moody, and the nuns purchased her house and 17 acres as a novitiate. Immediately they built a chapel, but it wasn't until 1949 that the rear three storey novitiate was finished.

In 1986, the nuns sold their Roebuck Castle Nursing Home to UCD. They then sold 31½ acres to builder, Dwyer Nolan, for £2.3million, who subsequently built Roebuck Castle housing estate. The nuns built the five storey Holy Family Residence in the grounds of Hermitage, for £8million, as a nursing home, with 80 en-suite rooms, catering largely for Health Board residents, and some priests. The nuns selling in 1986 were Julia Anne Fleming, Julia Corkery, Philomena Elizabeth Bolger, Anne O'Donoghue and Mary Anne Waldron. The nuns sold a further 3.23 acres at the rear in 2007, to Partenay Ltd (UCD), for an amazing €18 million, and the money is intended to be spent building a new nursing home for poor elderly in Waterford. This time the nuns selling were Kathleen Taylor, Kathleen McMahon, Mary Ward, and Ann Marie Kilmartin, all from Sybil Hill Convent in Raheny.

Internally the Holy Family Residence is very spacious, with the added benefit of a nice bright chapel on the first floor, lounges, dining rooms, a large occupational therapy room, and a hall for concerts, etc. Arranged visits from Mount Anville students are always a welcome treat. Some nuns still work here, in their white habit and headgear. Included in the building are 8 bedsits for active people.

The old house, Hermitage, is used for retreats for priests, and the nuns nowadays occupy the rear novitiate building as their convent, although their 1979 chapel is slightly remote from the main buildings.

The main block of Hermitage appears to be early 19th century, being three storey over basement and three bays wide. The original house may have been rectangular on plan, but around the middle of the 19th century, was possibly extended to the rear, creating a more square-shaped building. Certainly the exceptionally thick spine partition gives the impression that there might be two walls here. Various other wings were added over the years. Internally most rooms on all floor levels have ornate cornices and moulded door architraves, etc. The two interconnecting rear first floor rooms would have made a fine ballroom at one stage, greatly enhanced by the mock pillars and elaborate moulded architraves around the central opening.

The nuns were self sufficient, since they farmed the 17-acres, and also the larger estate of the adjoining Roebuck Castle, and no doubt exchanged ideas and help with the nearby Mount Anville nuns, also a French order.

Probably the most famous occupant from 1850 to 1920 was the Jameson family, of renowned whiskey fame. The 1901 Census listed John E. Jameson, aged 48, a distiller and Member of Parliament, living here together with his Scottish wife, five daughters and two sons, in addition to a nurse, a governess and four maids. The distillery started in the 1770's in Bow Street, Dublin (Smithfield), and closed in 1971, after which it became offices and a museum for the company. Another famous whiskey family, Haig, resided at one stage in the Roebuck area. Hermitage at one stage was occupied by the McCaskey family, who operated the Clonskeagh Iron Mill in the 1830's.

Hermitage – main house is on left of complex. and Novitiate on right. (LSOP)

Hermitage in 2006.

2007: Hermitage in foreground, German school on left, and UCD to rear. (PB)

Owenstown House

At the western end of Fosters Ave, partly concealed behind the former Foster Motors, is a plain late Georgian house, three bays wide, and two storeys over basement, with its back to Fosters Ave. The Turbett family, tea and wine merchants, were based here in the 19th century. Around 1930, George Plunkett leased the property, and almost immediatly bought it from the Irish Land Commission, who themselves had recently bought it from the Pembroke Estate. By 1938, his dairy herd consisted of 36 cows and 14 calves. Plunkett sold his 20 acres in 1943, and a small estate of houses was built after the War. Now the house is in office use, with a recent extension for apartments. There are some nice plaster cornices inside, together with lovely panelled doors and window shutters.

Owenstown House

Chapter 11

ST. THOMAS CHURCH

The Church of Ireland (Anglican) parish of Taney originally served the Mount Merrion area. However, some parishioners did not wish to make the journey to Taney Road church for all their needs, and so started Sunday evening services in 1859 in a cottage in the grounds of Seafield House on the Stillorgan Road, beside St. Helen's House. At that stage, Seafield was owned by a solicitor, Thomas Crozier.

In 1874, the church authorities agreed to the provision of a Chapel-of-Ease, at the bottom of Fosters Ave, calling it St. Thomas, although it was still part of Taney parish. The vestry on the south side was added in 1897 (converted in 1959 into an organ chamber), the north porch added in 1904, and the west baptistery added in 1965.

This small church is granite faced, and has a double pitched slated roof, and can accommodate about 160 people, thus making it very cosy and inviting, probably more suitable for prayer and meditation than a larger structure. There are many stained glass windows, which enrich the interior, including a pair behind the altar by L. Lobin of Tours (France), dating from 1875, two by A.E. Child, dated 1920, celebrating those who died (three) and survived The Great War (1914-1918), and two in memory of the Dudgeon family, who lived in Merville opposite the chapel. Other memorials include a marble life belt to Frederick Handy of Seafield, mosaic floor tiles in the aisle to Joseph Hume Dudgeon (of Merville), a brass plaque to Edward Percival Westby of Roebuck Castle (and County Clare), marble wall panels in memory of Mary Lady Nutting (of St. Helen's), a pulpit to Crozier (of Seafield), and a marble wall plaque to Turbett of Owenstown House. A 1941 stained glass window in the north porch is reputed to be by Evie Hone.

The Rev. Monk Gibbon was rector of Taney Parish from 1901 until his death in 1935, and the parishioners decided to build a hall to commemorate him. Hence the attractive Monk Gibbon Hall was opened in 1941, beside St. Thomas Church, and incorporates artificial stone dressings, and Killaloe slates. John du Moulin of Langlin, St. Thomas Road (later No. 45 Greygates) was the builder, and he later built the Church of St. Therese in Mount Merrion in 1956. The hall plot of land was leased to the church by Thomas Joseph Wilson for 500-years from 1926, whereas the church site is leased from the Earl of Pembroke. The hall is used by numerous clubs, and many concerts have been held here, although the stage is now gone. The hall was extended south in 1951, to provide a caretaker's flat and office. In 1953, a curate's residence was built just to the south of the church.

1956 was an important year, since the Chapel-of-Ease split from Taney parish, and became an independent Parish of Mount Merrion. The new Catholic Church of St. Therese was opened that same year.

Church of Ireland parishes normally have a graveyard beside the church, but in this case, most burials are in the other Chapel of Ease at St. Nathi, Dundrum. However, there are a few headstones around St. Thomas, and in recent years, a new Garden of Remembrance has been created in the south-east corner, where urns/ashes are deposited.

2006 view – church on left, rectory in centre, hall on right.

Interior of church, 2006.

117

Monk Gibbon Hall, 2006

Since 1994, St. Thomas parish has been grouped with St. Phillip and St. James in Cross Avenue, Booterstown, and Rev. Gillian Wharton is the current Rector of both.

Chapter 12

SOUTH HILL EVANGELICAL CHURCH

Tucked away in South Hill Park, a quiet cul-de-sac off the west end of Booterstown Ave, beside the former Shell Petrol Station on the Stillorgan Road, is a quaint little timber clad church, probably unknown to most Mount Merrionites. A branch of the Plymouth Brethren is based here, whose origins go back to Plymouth in England in the 1820's, and they practice a simple form of Christianity. There are no priests or ministers, although lay Elders usually lead the prayer service or bible reading. Members are baptised by full immersion in a sunken bath of water, usually when they are teenagers or adults, and fully aware of their faith and decision. This particular branch was established in a house in 1865, at No. 1 Anglesea Avenue, Blackrock. Other houses or "meeting houses" in the locality were also used, until the 1880's, when No. 22 Sydney Avenue became their permanent home, and the name Sydney Hall was adopted.

View in 2009

In 1953 they moved to South Hill Park, but still retained the name Sydney Hall until 1981, when the name South Hill Evangelical Church was adopted. The congregation is now very small, and their meetings are very informal and relaxed, more like a family get-together.

Interior of South Hill Evangelical Church.

Chapter 13

RADISSON BLU ST. HELEN'S HOTEL

Opened in 1998 as a 5-star Radisson Hotel, with 150 air-conditioned bedrooms in a modern extension, this property has an interesting history, dating back to the early 1750's, when Thomas Cooley, barrister and MP, built his house in open countryside on land belonging to the Fitzwilliam family, naming it Seamount, because of its high elevation overlooking the Dublin coastline. A map of 1783 shows Mrs Ford in occupation, although she was leasing it from Robert Alexander, Justice of the Peace, and High Sheriff of Dublin, and she was still there in 1830. John Doherty, MP and Lord Chief Justice of the Common Pleas, was the next occupier. The Rt Honourable Thomas F. Kennedy was in possession in the late 1830's, and he changed the name from Seamount to St Helens. Colonel Henry White was the occupier in the 1840's.

Around 1850, the property was acquired by Sir Hugh Gough, its most notorious occupant. From Woodstown, County Limerick, he joined the British Army in 1792 at the age of 13, and first gained recognition in Spain and Portugal during the Peninsular Wars (1808 – 1814). He was wounded at Talavera in Spain when the British were forced to retreat. He was pensioned off in 1815, but was later involved in quelling "unrest" in the Munster region of Ireland during the fight for Catholic Emancipation in the early 1820's. In the 1840's, he resumed his exploits, this time in India, but was no match for the Sikhs, and hence had to be replaced by Sir Charles Napier, after which he returned to Ireland and purchased St. Helens. Gough extended and altered St Helens in 1863, but he died in 1869, aged 90, and is buried in the family plot in St. Bridget's graveyard in Stillorgan (Church of Ireland). Because of its British Empire connotations, the Gough equestrian statue in the Phoenix Park was blown up in 1957, and stood on the main road near the Hollow (now a roundabout). The bronze statue, cast in London in 1880, was the work of acclaimed Irish artist, John Henry Foley (born in Foley Street, in inner-city Dublin), who also created the wonderful O'Connell monument in O'Connell Street. The Gough statue was restored, at great expense, and then sold by the Government in 1984, ending up in England two years later.

St. Helens then came into the hands of Sir John Nutting around 1899. In 1905, two years after he was made a Baronet, he clad the original brick facades with white Portland stone, and embellished the hall and ballroom with exquisite marbles. The original eaves was hidden behind a bottle balustrade, and the newly acquired Coat of Arms displayed on the front and rear pediment, comprising a half eagle-half lion enclosed between two nut branches, with the motto: "Mors Potior Macula" - "Death rather than Disgrace". The 1901 Census records that 48-year old John G. Nutting was a Protestant export merchant, and his son and daughter were present, aged 18 and 20 years respectively, plus a governess, and two young visitors. There were also two footmen, five house maids, two kitchen maids, one cook, one lady's maid, and two laundry maids. The main house had twenty four front windows, and forty rooms. There were eight other small cottages on the estate, occupied by two gardeners, two stable men, one herd, one butcher and one labourer. The outbuildings included two stables, one coach house, two harness rooms, one cow house, one calf house, one piggery, one barn, one potato house, one workshop, three sheds, one forge, one laundry, and one electric engine house.

The original estate was 93 acres, extending from the old Stillorgan Road to the Rock Road, and the magnificent mansion and estate was bought in 1924 by the Christian Brothers, as their Provincial headquarters and training Novitiate for new recruits. In conjunction with the Department of Education, they managed National Schools for boys, and various orphanages, such as Letterfrack in Co. Galway and Artane in Dublin. Almost immediately, the Brothers sold off about 19 acres abutting the Rock Road, where G & T Crampton Ltd built houses on St. Helen's Road in the early 1930's. These had three or four bedrooms, all with a garage, and with an average price tag of £1,085 each. By 1947, the Brothers had sold part of the sublet estate of San Soucci (but retained the stables) after which that house was demolished and a small estate of houses built. Sans Souci was once the home of the Digges La Touche family, famous Huguenot (French Protestant) bankers. The Pembroke Estate records that in 1830, William Digges LaTouche had a lease for 99 years from 1802, but had sublet to Robert Roe, and that the three-storey mansion was of the most superior class.

The late 1960's brought a sharp decline in "vocations" to the Christian Brothers, so the Novitiate moved to Bray, and St Helens was used only as the Provincialate. After moving to York Road in Dun Laoghaire in October 1988, they sold St Helens shortly afterwards to Rohan Commercial Properties, as agents for Phoenix Properties. The estate at this stage was 71 acres, but included 115 and 117, Booterstown Ave, which the Brothers had previously bought for the purpose of demolition and opening up the estate for development purposes. The Brothers obtained £5.15 million for the property, and the signatures on the contract were Jeremiah Columba Keating, Phillip Kevin Skehan, Cornelius Fidelius Horgan, and Thomas Peter Cronin.

Various developers/builders got involved in providing houses and apartments, including Fosterbrook, Seamount, Merrion Grove, Belfield Park, and St. Helen's Wood. The latter housing estate retained the old 1880's stables (from Sans Souci), and converted them into dwellings.

After buying it in 1996 from developer, Sean Dunne, Cosgrave Brothers restored St Helens House, and built a large bedroom wing, creating a lovely hotel. The large field in front of the hotel is now public open-space. The hotel is well worth a visit, to admire the marble floors and walls in the foyer, the lavish ballroom and organ gallery, and to stroll down the terraced gardens on the east side of the house. The library, now called La Panto Restaurant, features two beautiful carved oak fireplaces, copper overmantles depicting sailing ships, and beaten copper freeze. The Jacobbean room on the first floor (over the porch), is also interesting for its military-style decorations on the timber panelled walls. There is a portrait of Gough in the foyer.

Entrance Hall in Christian Brother's era. (IAA)

Present library

123

Rear Elevation (or was this the front?). (IAA)

"A healthy mind in a healthy body". (CBS)

During the Christian Brothers era. (CBS)

Ballroom of St Helens used as chapel in CBS era. (IAA)

125

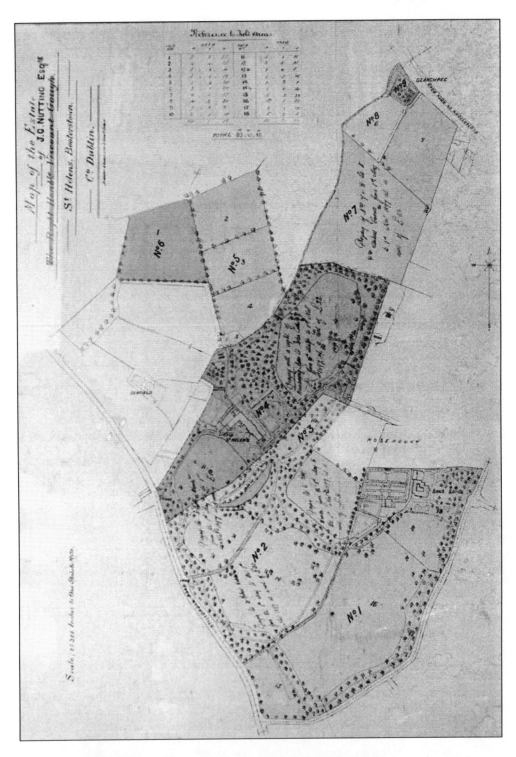

**St Helens Estate – Stillorgan Road along bottom left, Booterstown Avenue
along bottom right, and Rock Road at top right (IAA)**

1956: Notice the orangery on right of house, novitiate to left of house, glasshouses and garden to left, and handball alley amongst the trees. (NL)

Chapter 14

CATHOLIC COMMUNICATIONS CENTRE

When Ireland's first television station, Telefis Eireann, opened on New Year's Eve, 1961, alarm bells rang in Archbishop McQuaid's palace in Drumcondra. He feared that the Catholic church would lose control over the everyday lives of Irish people, with lurid and scandalous English and American programmes being beamed directly into the livingrooms of every family in the country, and corrupting innocent minds! Initially only the wealthy could afford to buy TV sets, but then the hire companies allowed the ordinary people to rent TVs from week to week.

McQuaid's office compiled a detailed dossier on the high-ranking staff in RTE, noting that only 4 of the 16 producers were Catholic, and of these only two were practicing. Black marks were awarded against them, because they were either liberal, trade unionist, graduates of Trinity College (perceived as exclusively Protestant), had visited Russia, were English, converts, divorced, admirers of Joyce or Yeats, had worked previously with the Irish Times (another Protestant flagship), or were former IRA internees in the Curragh Camp during World War Two. Another invasive dossier prepared in 1962 had reservations about eleven senior staff members (or their guests), who were members of the Irish Workers League, with particular emphasis on the "Broadsheet" programme. Taboo subjects for McQuaid were the Common Market (now the EU), NATO, and Communism. He regarded the Irish Nuclear Disarmament movement as Communist sponsored, and the Fabian Society in Trinity College as a Communist cell. The 1913 Club was looked upon as an extreme left-wing group in Dublin. McQuaid continued to monitor the personnel in RTE, and the content of programmes, and frequently tried to interfere in the running of the station. Even the lay Catholic organization, the Knights of St. Columbanus, organized "Look/Listen" groups in 1965, and reported their findings to McQuaid.

People these days might not remember that Telefis Eireann was initially Black and White (i.e. no colour!), and it's daily programme started at 5.30 in the evening, and closed at 11.30 P.M., when everyone went to bed. The Late Late Show was hosted by Gay Byrne on Saturday night, from 10.55 to 12 midnight.

However, even before the arrival of RTE, the Irish Catholic church was aware of the power of broadcasting. The Dublin Institute of Catholic Sociology, 14,

Gardiner Place, whose patron was McQuaid, was sending priests to ABC Television in Manchester, England, for a special religious broadcasting training course. Father Joseph Dunn, a curate in Rialto, went on the one-week course in June 1959. In September 1959, Fr. Joseph Dunn and Fr. Des Forristal were sent to the Academy of Broadcasting Arts in New York, to do a three month course in broadcasting. By 1961, Joseph Dunn was in the UCD Chaplaincy, 84, St. Stephen's Green, and was sent to Antwerp in Belgium, in company with Fr. Des Forristal, Fr. Peter Lemass and Fr. Donal Flavin, to do a course in film making. Des Forristal and Joseph Dunn immediately began making short documentary films with a religious flavour, and persuaded the recently opened RTE to screen their first edition of Radharc on 12th January 1962.

On 10th August 1963, Dunn was appointed Chaplin in the Dominican Convent, 123 Mount Merrion Avenue, to facilitate his work in making the Radharc films for RTE. Initially RTE paid Dunn £125 per episode, but RTE assisted in processing the film, etc. They increased the fee to £250 by 1964. In 1965, McQuaid granted Dunn permission to make films in Africa.

The Church now saw the need for a purpose built Catholic Communications Centre, and so the Catholic Truth Society of Ireland (founded in 1899) bought three acres of land for £11,100 from the Christian Brothers estate of St. Helens, at the corner of the Stillorgan Road and Booterstown Avenue. The new centre opened in 1967, having been built for £54,000, including equipment, and provided 8-week courses in religious broadcasting. Dunn was its first director, but he continued to produce Radharc films for RTE as a separate business.

In 1969, the Catholic Communications Centre amalgamated with the Catholic Truth Society to form the Catholic Communications Institute of Ireland, with the publishing arm in Veritas House, 7-8, Lower Abbey Street, Dublin, from 1970.

In 1970, the CCII bought nearby Pranstown House on 1.5 acres (on the other side of Booterstown Ave beside South Hill Park) for £24,250. This house was previously called Temora, and comprised 4 reception rooms, 5 bedrooms, 2 bathrooms, servants quarters, a double garage, and even a heated greenhouse. Dunn and his Radharc crew moved into Pranstown House. However, by 1974, Dublin County Council compulsory acquired part of the property for £150,000 for road widening purposes, and later demolished the old house. Irish Nationwide Building Society bought the rest of the land from the CCII in 1977, and completed a large block of apartments there in 2008, called Booterstown Wood, although they were not put on the market (at half price) until October 2010.

The first director of the Communications Centre was Fr. Joseph Dunn, followed by Fr. Peter Lemass, and then Bunny Carr. Besides offering broadcasting courses to priests, and making Radharc films, the centre also made promotional films for Trocaire and Gorta, both church sponsored overseas aid agencies, and also for various missionary orders. In fact, Trocaire was based in the centre in Booterstown. The accounts for the period 1969-71, showed that RTE paid the centre £11,288, and other organizations paid £8,845.

Peter Lemass died in 1988, and Joseph Dunn in 1996, at which stage, Radharc ended, after making more than 400 films, both in Ireland and around the world. However, the films can still be purchased from Esras, at 43, Mount Merrion Ave, which manages the collection on behalf of the Irish Film Archive and Radharc Trust.

Bunny Carr is probably the most famous lay person associated with running the centre. He then started his own company, Carr Communications, in 1973, which specialized in grooming politicians and business people for television appearances, especially the Late Late Show. After Radharc ceased production in 1996, Carr Communications moved into the refurbished Communications Centre, and stayed until 2004, when there was a Management Buyout, and the company moved to Sandyford Industrial Estate. However, most people probably associate Bunny Carr as a broadcaster on RTE, when he fronted the afternoon show called Going Strong, from 1975 – 1983, and Quicksilver, from 1980 (a quiz show with low prize money).

Terry Prone and her husband, Tom Savage, were other personalities associated with Carr Communications, but they left in early 2008, after twenty five years service, to start a new venture.

Now the Booterstown site of the former Catholic Communications Centre has been cleared, and high rise blocks of apartments have been built there, called Thorn Wood. However, the book publishing arm is still going strong as Veritas in Lower Abbey Street, although its branch shop in Stillorgan village closed a few years ago, and is now occupied by the Blood Transfusion Service. The Catholic Communications Centre is now based in Maynooth Seminary/College in Co. Kildare. The Booterstown site had been sold by the Church in 2002 for €7.618 million to Charles and Edmund O'Reilly Hyland.

**Pranstown House in the 1970's at top of Booterstown Ave
(now Booterstown Wood apartments).** (DLR)

CCC in 2006 (now Thorn Wood apartments).

Chapter 15

COLAISTE EOIN - COLAISTE IOSAGAIN

Colaiste Eoin

This All-Irish Secondary school for Boys is owned by the Christian Brothers, and the land was part of St. Helen's Estate, the Provincialate and Novitiate of the Brothers. They started a school in prefabs in 1969, beside St. Helen's House, and built the present single storey school in 1975. At present the school caters for 440 boys, and 28 teachers are employed.

Colaiste Iosagain

This All-Irish Secondary school for Girls is owned by the Sisters of Mercy, but is built on Christian Brother's land, immediately alongside the Secondary School for Boys, Colaiste Eoin. The girl's school started in Carysfort Avenue in 1971, but moved to the Stillorgan Road in 1984, to a new single storey building. 460 girls are taught by 30 teachers.

In 2003, €9 million was spent on a new four storey school block, and separate sports hall/concert hall. These new school buildings are partly shared by the boys and girls in 5th and 6th years from the two original school buildings.

The hall has an unusual concave shaped roof, with wide overhanging eaves, but the overall external appearance is possibly spoiled by the brown coloured props under the eaves, which give the impression of temporary emergency holding devices.

The original single-storey blocks for both schools are arranged around the four sides of a courtyard, which acts as a good play and meeting area, the nearest thing to co-education.

The complex of buildings is separated from the Stillorgan Road by a playing field. There is a new small outside hand ball alley beside the rear hall.

2006: New hall on left, old school in front, new school at rear.

Typical modern classroom

Chapter 16

STILLORGAN PARK HOTEL

Mount Merrion House, the Irish seat of the Fitzwilliam/Pembroke family, was the "big house" in the locality, but another late-Georgian property on the east side of Stillorgan Road also aspired to grandeur, and was given a similar name, although had only a small plot of land. The original three bay two storey over basement house was extended on both sides, probably in the late 19th Century, thereby making it quite imposing and very visible from the main road. In fact, although the house itself was on the Fitzwilliam estate, the rear plot of land was on Lord Carysfort's estate. The 1901 Census records 40-year old William Brudenell Murphy, a landlord, living there with his wife, son and daughter, together with a cook, house maid, kitchen maid, butler, groom, and gardener. There were twenty front windows, thirty rooms, and ten out offices (stables, sheds, etc.). The Murphy family ownership extended back a few generations, but by the 1930's the house had changed hands, and in fact, the north wing was separated and renamed Hopetown House.

Pascal Vincent Doyle (or P.V. as he was more commonly known) heralded in the swinging 60's, when Jack Lynch, Minister for Industry and Commerce, opened P.V.'s small South County Hotel in June 1961. P.V. was born in 1923, and started his building career working for his father's company, Frankfort Estates, in Dundrum. P.V. built houses in the 1950's, such as beside Terenure College, Orwell Road, Fortfield Road, St Brigids in Clonskeagh. His first big project was the County Club in Churchtown in the late 1950's (later called the Braemor Rooms, and then McGowans). Next, he bought Hopetown, the north wing of Mount Merrion House, and some land attached, and built a detached two storey hotel, called the South County Hotel. Hopetown (Holdings) Ltd. was the company involved, and the 7-day drinks licence was transferred from a Cork pub. There were 20 bedrooms on the first floor (no ensuites), while the ground floor was laid out as a lounge with corner bar, a much larger central cocktail cum coffee lounge (the Green Room), a diningroom, kitchen and small residents lounge. A special feature was the 62' x 22' open air swimming pool at the rear of the hotel. There was a massive 22" TV in the reception, and an 80' high aerial on the roof. Bed and breakfast cost 32s.6d, and you could enjoy a four-course lunch for 5s.6d in the Steak Grill. Saturday evening dances were very popular. Within a year, P.V. had sold the hotel to Irish Cinemas Ltd/Rank Organization for £100,000, and went on to bigger and better hotels, such as the Montrose in 1964, the Burlington in 1970, and eventually built up Ireland's most famous hotel chain. Incidentally, Irish Cinemas Ltd, so long associated with the Elliman Brothers, closed down the famous Theatre Royal in Hawkins Street in 1961, thus ending the wonderful days of a variety show combined with a film.

The South County was extended in 1965, at a cost of £180,000, and could now boast of 70 centrally-heated bedrooms, with telephone, shower, some private baths, in addition to a Merrion Suite with seating capacity of 300, suitable for wedding breakfasts. Bed and breakfast was now £7.

In the 1970's, the hotel had mixed fortunes, and even lost its drinks licence from November 1974 to May 1975. Then it re-opened, and heralded in the disco era. However, further changes were afoot, and the exotic Parkes Hotel opened in 1982, comprising the 4,500 square ft lounge/bar called Coconut Grove, the 2,500 square ft Peppermint Garden Restaurant, and the 8,500 square ft. Flamingos Night Club. There were 40 double/twin bedrooms, and 7 staff rooms, all ensuite. This venue was really glamorous and lively, and even featured "bunny girls". Rock Fox and his jazz band performed here regularly.

In 1987, Parkes Hotel was sold for £2 million to businessman Sean Quinn, after the demolition of the old Mount Merrion House, which still stood, all boarded up, between the hotel building and the Texaco garage. The hotel, now called the Stillorgan Park Hotel, went into decline, including the night club, and by 1996, the Pettit family from Wexford bought it, and practically rebuilt and greatly enlarged the property, upgrading it to 4 Star status, catering largely for conferences, weddings and coach tours, utilizing the 165 air conditioned bedrooms. The present large reception/foyer, large Turf Club bar/lounge, and Purple Sage restaurant, have very colourful and lively décor and furnishings, with emphasis on yellow and purple, the official colours of the Wexford football and hurling team, who have made the hotel their base when occasionally playing in Croke Park.

P.V. built up a hotel empire, but sadly passed to his eternal reward in 1988, aged 65. Taoiseach, Charlie Haughey, led the tributes at the funeral, and recalled P.V.'s generosity. His lifelike portrait still hangs in many Dublin hotels.

Devotees of the pop star, Def Leppard, will no doubt have enjoyed the 1986 album, Hysteria, and in particular the track, Pour Some Sugar on Me. The accompanying video shows the band playing amidst the shell of Mount Merrion House, while it was actually being demolished by a "ball and chain".

South County Hotel, 1961. (Irish Times)

South County Hotel, 1965

Parkes Hotel, 1987 (was called South County Hotel). (FiMe)

Present Stillorgan Park Hotel

Mount Merrion House in the 1980's. Hopetown, the north wing, was still occupied. (IAA)

1970's forecourt looking south. (DLR)

1970's: South County Hotel forecourt on right. On rear left is the Esso garage/showrooms, and Pembroke lodge to south of garage. (DLR)

March 1963: Notice the open-air swimming pool to the side of the South County Hotel. Mount Merrion House/Hopewell House to right of Hotel., and recent Texaco Garage. Keegans Farm to rear of Hotel. Gleesons Garage (now Esso) to front left, including Pembroke Estate lodge. (NL)

Chapter 17

MOUNT MERRION PITCH AND PUTT CLUB

Very few people know about this nicely landscaped oasis behind the Stillorgan Park Hotel, accessed via a lane alongside No. 7, Priory Avenue, which is probably Mount Merrion's best kept secret.

Back in the 18th Century, large tracks of land around here were part of the Carysfort estate.

Stillorgan Priory was a grand Victorian house located roughly between the Pitch and Putt Club and Priory Drive. It may have taken its name from a real priory, since the 1837 Ordnance Survey map shows "priory ruins" around the present Stillorgan VEC College on the old Dublin Road. In the mid 19th Century, the Sweetman family occupied the house, and then the Dudgeon family occupied it from about 1872 – 1925, after which it was abandoned. The many gables on the house may have inspired the Keegan family to name their nearby house/farm as The Gables.

Just after the Second World War (the Emergency in Ireland!), various builders, including Sisk and McInerney, developed the Priory Housing Estate, leaving 2 acres, 1 rood and 39 perches as public open space, which quickly became a dumping ground.

The Church of St. Therese in Mount Merrion was on the lookout for a site for tennis courts, and leased the open space in 1958 from Hardwicke Ltd. However, the cost of the project was too high, and the land was left idle. The Pope's Second Vatican Council was convened in 1962, and advocated greater communication with the other Christian churches (Ecumenism). Hence, from 1964 onwards, the Catholics, Anglicans and Presbyterians around Mount Merrion, organized an annual golf outing to different clubs, such as the Grange in Rathfarnham, Foxrock, etc. This led to the idea of a Pitch and Putt Club for the young people of Mount Merrion, and the Priory open space was chosen as the location. The land was cleared and landscaped, and the small pavilion built for meetings, mostly by voluntary effort, but with some fundraising. The official opening and Catholic blessing occurred in 1967, including an exhibition game by the Irene Club and CYMS, organized by the Pitch and Putt Union of Ireland.

The club was owned by trustees – Fr. Rogers of St. Therese Church, Tom Murray of Sycamore Road, and John Shanahan of Priory Avenue. The first captain in 1967/1968 was Jack Deignan.

In 1978, the landlord, Hardwicke Ltd. wanted to lay sewers across the Pitch and Putt course in order to facilitate development of lands to the south of the hotel. Hence a Wayleave Agreement was signed by Joseph Kilroy and Nigel Kennedy on behalf of the club, in favour of Michael Kelly and Padraig MacGinty. In exchange, the club was granted outright ownership of the property, and by deed dated 31st December 1979, Hardwicke Ltd. sold the freehold to Neil Kennedy of The Rise, and Joseph Kilroy of High Park Avenue, Blackrock. Neil and Joe were club captains in 1973 and 1974 respectively.

Because of its small size, the nine holes are very easy to get around, and half an hour is usually enough. Some of the old estate stone boundary walls can still be seen along part of the south and west sides.

Nowadays the club is run by a president, vice president, honorary vice president, a captain, vice captain, honorary secretary, honorary treasurer, and an 11 member committee, mostly elderly. The 2010 Captain is Arthur Smith, and the 2010/2011 President is Bob Lee. Membership costs €50 per annum, which seems like great value if it includes insurance, grass cutting, etc. However, the club is very exclusive, and seems to have lost sight of the original purpose of the club, i.e. as an outlet for young people. The Mount Merrion Ecumenical Golf Society, involving clergy from the three Christian churches in the area (Anglican, Catholic, and Presbyterian) is still going strong, and in 2010 had their annual get-together in the Woodbrook Golf Club.

In times past, the area to the north of the Priory Estate was in the townland of Woodlands, and in fact, various old maps show a lot of trees around here. After the Second World War, an exclusive housing estate called Woodland Park was developed, and a special feature of most garden gates is a white painted steel cut out in the shape of different furry animals, such as rabbits, foxes, squirrels, etc.

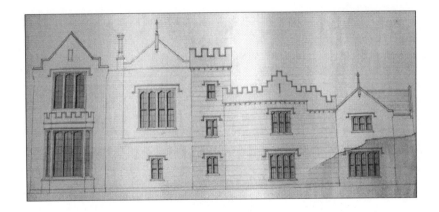

Priory House: 1872 alterations (staff quarters) for Henry Dudgeon. (IAA)

Priory House before demolition. (MMPP)

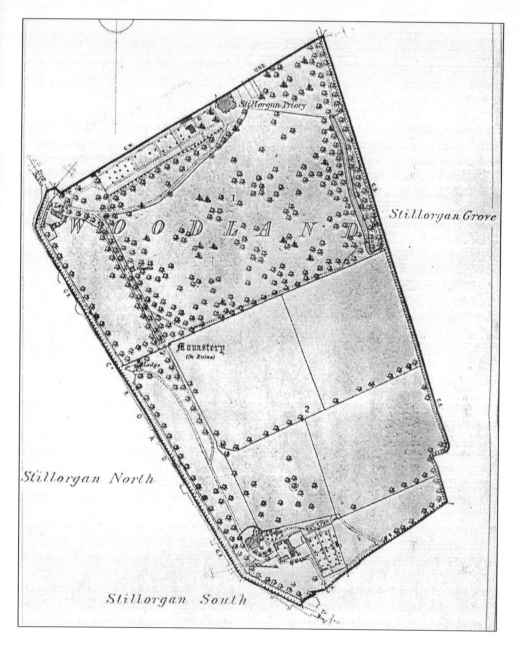

Lagrange estate, 1881 - Grove House at the bottom was later called Tigh Lorcain Hall (the Irish for Stillorgan is Teach Lorgan – the House of St Lawrence), and was demolished to make way for Leisureplex, after a dairy farm was bought by the County Council in the early 1950's, in preparation for the Stillorgan by-pass.
The present pitch and putt club is immediately to the north of Stillorgan Priory.
(NA1, LEC rental 141/29)

143

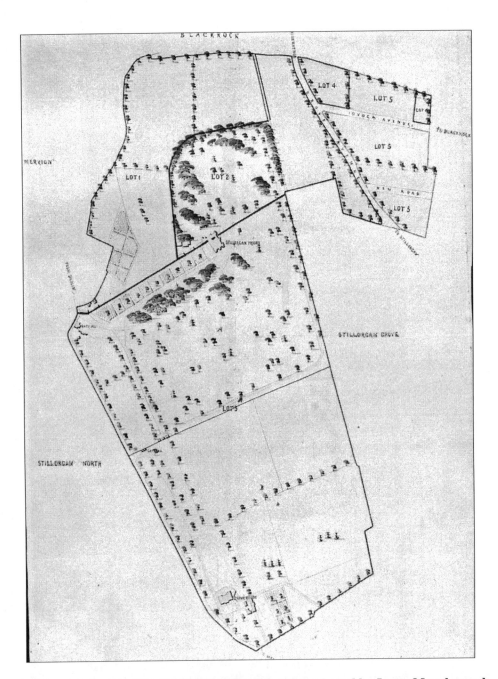

1860 map of Woodland for Earl of Carysfort. Lot 1 was leased by James Murphy, and adjoined his house, Mount Merrion, on the Fitzwilliam estate. Lot 2 and 3a comprised Stillorgan Priory, and leased by P. Sweetman for 99 years from 1784. Lot 3b comprising Grove House, was leased by G. Hughes. Lot 4 was building ground, leased by J.J Verschoyle. Lot 5 was building ground occupied by Lord Carysfort. Lot 6 was building ground leased by G. Stormont. Mount Merrion Avenue now runs along the top of the map from left to right. (NA1)

144

Chapter 18

SOUTH HILL

The Dominican order in Ireland (once enclosed) can trace its origins to Galway in 1644, but by 1717, Mary Bellew and a few other nuns, came to an existing convent in Channel Row (present North Brunswick Street) in Dublin, to found a boarding school for young ladies. This lovely detached convent had previously been occupied by the Poor Clare nuns, and was four storeys high, with a large garden and a separate chapel. The Dominicans stayed in Channel Row until about 1808, when they moved to Clontarf. By 1820, Clontarf was closed and the nuns had bought a house in Cabra, which is still their Motherhouse today. The nuns established Sion Hill School at the bottom of Mount Merrion Avenue in 1836, at which stage there were 8 boarders, 10 nuns and 40 day pupils.

In 1959, the nuns acquired No. 123, Mount Merrion Avenue, better known as South Hill House, a late Georgian mansion on 9 acres, to be used as a Hall of Residence for university students, in preparation for the impending move of UCD to nearby Belfield. The house they bought included a two storey gate lodge, a two storey gardener's house, a battery hen house, a cow house (two tyings), stables with five stalls, a two car garage, a walled garden with four large glasshouses, in addition to the usual tennis courts. The house was re-named Rosaryville.

The builders, John Sisk & Son Ltd., set to work in late 1963, on a modern three storey extension, which opened in October 1965, providing 38 study-bedrooms, and the property was then re-named Dominican Hall. The university hostel closed in 1967, and then became the Novitiate, called St Dominics, to which a further wing was added in 1968. In 1976, the Novitiate moved to 47 Mount Merrion Avenue, and their former premises became the Generalate for the Dominicans.

In 1987, the entire property was sold, after which a developer demolished the modern block to make way for a nice estate of 60-townhouses, while retaining the period house, South Hill. The former gateway from Mount Merrion Avenue is still there, with a new house built on the driveway, and the former two-storey gate lodge restored. The former rear entrance from Booterstown Avenue is still in place, as evidenced by a pair of brown timber gates at the end of a row of 1930's slated houses.

South Hill is two storey over basement, with various large extensions. The stained glass conservatory on the shallow first floor return features portraits of three ladies, and small birds – the latter are also included at the top of various front windows.

William Harvey du Cross, who was involved with John Dunlop in the development of the pneumatic tyre, lived here from around 1890-1905. Earlier occupiers of the house included Charles Hopes and William Pennefather. The nuns purchased the house from the Hannan family, wholesale drapers in Abbey Street, who themselves bought the house in the early 1940's.

Many people will be interested to learn that the famous British author, Neville Shute, lived here as a teenager from 1912 to 1915. His proper name is Neville Shute Norway, but he only used his surname in business life as an aeronautical engineer, and his two Christian names as his pen-name. He was born in England in 1899, and moved to South Hill in 1912, when his father, Arthur Norway, was appointed head of the Post Office in Ireland, based in the GPO. The family leased South Hill, and could afford to employ three servants, a gardener and a young assistant. Neville still attended private school in England, and came to Ireland during school holidays. The Norways left South Hill in the autumn of 1915 after their other son Fred died in France a few months earlier, during the First World War, and went to live in the Royal Hibernian Hotel, Dawson Street. On the morning of Easter Monday 1916, Arthur Norway had some overtime to do, and went into his office in the GPO. However, he was immediatly summoned to Dublin Castle, and instructed to cut off all phones and telegraph lines to Munster, because of suspicious Volunteer activities in Kerry. During Arthurs absence from the GPO, it was taken over by Padraig Pearse, and the rest is history. As it happened, young Neville was making his way from the Royal Hibernian Hotel to the GPO to visit his father, and he witnessed the start of the Easter Rising. While at school in England all the young lads were trained in civil defence, so Neville enlisted with the Royal Irish Automobile Club in Dawson Street, as a stretcher bearer in their makeshift ambulances. After the Rising, the Norways were posted back to England, and an Irishman appointed to head the Post Office.

The early development of South Hill Demesne makes interesting reading, as it formed part of the Fitzwilliam Estate. In 1802, Viscount Fitzwilliam let 13 acres to John Verschoyle (his Agent), including an existing house. The following year, John Verschoyle and his wife Barbara, sublet 8 acres to Michael Farrell, and the new lease included a covenant to build a house for at least £500 (Lot No 1 on map). The other 5 acres were leased to John Radcliffe (Lot 2-9). Samuel Pittar, a developer/builder, then acquired the leases. In the next three decades, Pittar had rebuilt South Hill (it can be clearly seen on Duncan's map of 1821), created South Hill Avenue to link Mount Merrion Avenue and Booterstown Avenue, and then built many more villas and houses, such as Arbutus Lodge, Netley, St. Aubyns, South Hill Cottage, Hamilton Cottage, Marmion Lodge (now Oak Lodge), Rokeby, in addition to Talbot House and Hungerford House, and Eden Ville Terrace (all of which can be seen on the 1837 Ordnance Survey map). The houses were let to different tenants, often on yearly leases, and in effect were like a modern investment portfolio. However, by 1855, the Landed Estates Court sold the entire portfolio to Edmond Percival Morphy, but in 1866, the Court was again forced to sell the properties on behalf of Morphy's widow, and at that stage, South Hill House was let to Dr. James Apjohn, for 21-years from 1857 (he was an eminent Professor of Chemistry and Mineralology at Trinity College).

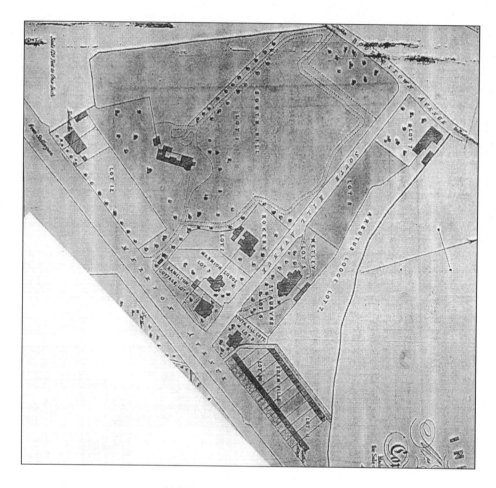

1866 Plan. (NA1, LEC rental 34/80)

147

1986 aerial view of South Hill. (PB)

1986 aerial of South Hill – notice the lean-to glasshouses on bottom left. (PB)

South Hill. (DN)

148

South Hill. (DN)

Order of St Camillus, South Hill Avenue

Three-storey Netley was built in the early decades of the 19th century, and was semi-detached from St Aubyns. The house came into the possession of this Italian order in the early 1980's, for use by the chaplain to St Lukes Hospital, Rathgar. The order set up in Ireland in 1935, to cater for the sick, and they still operate a Nursing Home in Killucan, Co Westmeath. They also act as chaplains to the Mater Hospital in Dublin, living in a nearby house.

Ashurst

At the western top end of Mount Merrion Ave stood a two storey three bay house, called Palermo. This was acquired around 1900 by an architect called Caldbeck, who extended it to the rear, and also added an extra rear storey. In the 1940's/50's, the house was owned by Conor Alexander Maguire, President of the Supreme Court. His son, Conor Patrick, was a circuit Court judge, although in retirement, he worked for RTE radio in the 1990's, presenting the popular jazz programme, "In the Mood". In 1961, the house was acquired by Irish Telephone Rentals, a British company which rented out telephone systems for offices. They demolished the old house around 1975, and built a modern office block, complete with its own telephone exchange. The company moved to Tallaght in 1990, and are now part of Cable and Wireless. The new owners of the Mount Merrion Ave building leased it to M.C. O'Sullivan, Consulting Engineers. The office block was demolished in 2005, and a block of apartments built, Merrion Hall.

Meanwhile, the front garden of the old house was sold to hotelier/builder P.V.Doyle, who initially planned a hotel for the site, but changed his mind, and in 1972 he built a block of 55 flats, "Ashurst", for rental only. In the last decade or so, renting has ceased, and one by one, the flats have been sold to individuals.

Fortwilliam on left, Ashurst on right (Stillorgan Road behind both). (Aerofilms)

Fortwilliam

Across the road from Ashurst, on the opposite side of Mount Merrion Avenue, was another, though smaller, old house, which was demolished in the late 1970's to make way for apartments. However, the coach house, which was right behind the main house, survives, having been converted into a charming residence at some earlier stage, called Fortwilliam Cottage, with access directly off the Stillorgan Road. It was sold in 2007, and awaits the bulldozer.

Rear of Fortwilliam

150

Chapter 19

Shops and Businesses

Mount Merrion Gardens

Few will remember this name, and might be surprised to learn that it was, in fact, a terrace of shops on the main Stillorgan Road, where Priory Hall offices now stand. These shops were built in 1935 to cater for the newly emerging Mount Merrion Estate houses. It must also be remembered that the main Stillorgan Road was much narrower than today, and had very little traffic up until the early 1970's. Prior to the advent of supermarkets in the 1960's, people walked to the local shops every day, buying fresh meat in one, vegetables in another, etc. In addition, the big bakeries delivered fresh loaves of bread daily to your house (there was no sliced bread!), while milk bottles were left on your doorstep early every morning, after you had left out the empty glass pint bottles the night before.

1970's, looking north (now Priory Hall). The Gables on right (Keegans Farm). (DLR)

151

1964: Priory Drive on right. No dual-carriageway yet. (NL)

The range of shops in Mount Merrion Gardens in 1965 gives a good idea of the services available, bearing in mind that Ireland's first shopping centre, in Stillorgan, wasn't opened until the following year. First was, Bain, the chemist, followed by Mc Garry, newsagent and tobacconist. Then you had Mc Donagh, the butcher, and Lennon, shoe repairs. In those days, you didn't throw away your old shoes – you had them "soled and heeled", making them nearly new again. The famous Findlaters occupied two shops, and you bought all your groceries here. Everything was stocked on shelves behind a long counter, behind which stood the grocer, and he took your shopping list (or you shouted out what you wanted), and filled your leather or canvas shopping bag with your packets of loose tea leaves, bags of sugar, biscuits, eggs, jam, cheese etc. Your slices of ham, cornbeef, and haslett were cut on the spot. Sometimes you didn't pay that day, but your account was noted in a big ledger, and you "cleaned your slate" on Friday, payday. Findlaters had a branch here (one of many throughout Dublin, mostly larger) from 1950 to 1968. Next to Findlaters was the Royal Bank of Ireland, and beyond that, Miss Lennon, the sweetshop. Gerald Keegan occupied The Gables next door, and finally, Swiss Cleaners, dry cleaners.

The two-storey shops were brick-faced, arranged in pairs, with a flat roofed side wing, including a garage, and the first floor apartment had three bedrooms, livingroom, kitchen, bathroom, and toilet.

Texaco in 1970's looking south. (DLR)

153

To the north of Mount Merrion Gardens was Mount Merrion Motors Ltd (later called Safety Service Station, and recently Texaco), who were main dealers for Opel and NSU, and had over 50 used cars for sale. Some readers will remember the NSU Prinz 4, an early 1960's model. In those happy days, the garage stayed open until 10.00 pm each evening (6.00 pm on Saturday). Now the garage workshops are used by a vending machine company, and the forecourt is a builders storage yard. The timber lattice roof trusses in the building are a noteworthy feature, both segmental and triangular.

Included in Mount Merrion Gardens was a premises called The Gables, bought in 1938 by the Keegans. This in fact was a farmhouse, with six acres attached. Prior to this, the Keegans sold their Swift car distribution business in St Stephens Green, which also supplied all the timber framed vans for Bewleys coffee. Keegans fields accommodated a few cows, but their main business was pigs (about 100), and around 4,000 caged battery hens, in addition to some market gardening (potatoes etc). The new N11 in the late 1970's heralded the demisc of Keegans, when Mount Merrion Gardens was Compulsorily Purchased by the County Council, and then demolished. In 1990, the shop site and part of Keegans fields, was developed by Guardian Builders, as Priory Hall, comprising about 2,700 sq. metres of offices in two three-storey blocks, subdivided into small own-door office units, in addition to a central two storey car park. Then in the mid 1990's the last parcel of land was developed as Treesdale, an estate of 41 houses. Parts of the old high stone boundary wall between Keegans and the former Stillorgan Priory can still be seen around Treesdale (see chapter on Pitch and Putt club).

Just down the road from Mount Merrion Gardens was Ashurst Garage, a Fiat dealer, and until recently a Shell petrol station. A new Applegreen petrol station was built in early 2010. Irish Shell and BP Ltd, owned The Chequered Flag garage on Deerpark Road, next door to the present Flanagans Furniture.

Shell garage in the 1970's (now Applegreen). (DLR)

154

At the bottom of The Rise was Greygates Filling Station, which in the 1950's sold caravans, such as a Shannon model for £385. This was replaced by a block of apartments in 2001, Fitzwilliam Court.

Diagonally across from Mount Merrion Gardens was Noel E. Gleeson Ltd., a Volkswagen dealer, and Esso petrol retailer. Noel lived in the house on the north side of the garage, called Dandenong. The garage, including two small shops, was built in 1935, at the same time as the Greygates houses, and was originally owned by Eames, and called Estate Garage (it is still called Estate Service Station). Noel, a rally car driver, acquired the business in the early 1950's, and expanded it in the 1960's by setting up the Stillorgan Ambulance Service. He had five private ambulances on the road, operating from Stillorgan to Wexford, including Dublin's only cardiac ambulance, the latter catering for about ten patients a week. In the late 1970's, Esso acquired and demolished Gleesons, introducing the modern canopied forecourt, which has undergone several changes in appearance since then. Esso started in Ireland in 1898 as the Anglo American Oil Co., selling paraffin oil for house lamps (before the widespread use of gas and then electricity for domestic needs), but by 1910 was selling petrol (Pratts Perfection Spirits) for the newly arrived mass produced motor car. The company changed its name to Esso in 1935, and went on to fame and fortune with its Esso Blue (paraffin oil), and its advertising campaign entitled "Put a Tiger in your Tank". The company had its headquarters just past Stillorgan village, from 1962 to 2002, after which The Grange apartment blocks were built.

On the south side of Gleesons forecourt was a single storey cottage, which was demolished by Esso in 1981. This was a gate lodge for the Fitzwilliam/Pembroke demesne, alongside a diagonal avenue leading to the farmyard. The lodge had granite random rubble walls, with cut quoins, brick window dressings, and slated roof. The last occupier was Miss O'Connor.

Esso in 1970's - note the Mount Merrion House lodge on left. (DLR)

155

Noel Gleeson Ltd (now Esso Garage)

The Rise

A small collection of shops was built on The Rise in the mid 1930's as part of John Kenny's estate, including a grocers shop. John Meagher was the original main grocery shop, superceded by H. Williams in the 1950's, and this company later developed into a famous supermarket chain. The Mount Merrion branch then became a Super-Valu outlet in the 1980's, which continues to expand on the site. These days, the other shops include a newsagent cum post office, a chemist, a small flower shop, and a small drycleaners.

Further up The Rise is No 93, a small estate of offices, now leased by Biotrin International, a diagnostics company specialising in tests for infectious diseases. John Du Moulin owns the estate, and used it in earlier decades as his builders yard, especially when he built the new Catholic church in 1956. The two storey offices are stone built, with slated roofs, and date from the mid 18th century, when they comprised the stables for Mount Merrion House. The north wing was demolished in the 1970's by the parish priest after an earlier fire, but you can still see some parts of a wall, at the rear of the Scout Hall.

The Rise, 2006

Deerpark Road

A substantial group (in fact, two groups) of shops was built in the early 1960's, and the newsagent, Ed McGuire, is still going strong, and much loved by all children in the area, because of his "penny sweets". Nowadays, there is a furniture shop, a chemist, a butcher, a florist/greengrocer, a hairdresser, a ladies boutique, a wine/deli cum restaurant, in addition to various offices above the shops.

2006 views of Deerpark Road

Trees Road Upper

A small group of shops was built in the early 1960's, and nowadays, there are two ladies hairdressers, a chic café, a grocer, chemist, solicitor, and bicycle/lawnmower shop.

Trees Road, 2006

Glenville Industrial Estate, 26 Fosters Avenue

This estate, comprising about an acre of land, is a secluded low-rise terrace of factory buildings, dating from the early 1960's, which were partly occupied by Smith and Nephew - Southalls (Ireland) Ltd, probably for warehousing, and later by RTE to store props etc.

Motor Import Ltd also occupied part of the estate from 1967 to 1973, and in fact, this is where the story of BMW cars in Ireland began. Frank Keane was the General Manager of Mount Merrion Motors (later called Texaco Garage) in the early 1960's, and after a spell with the Three Rock Garage in Rathfarnham, started his own company, with two co-directors, importing this luxury car from Germany, and selling them through approved car dealers. Bayerische Motoren Werke (Bavarian Motor Works) is located in Munich. The first models, including the top end Tilux, ranged from 1.6 to 2.0 litres, with prices of £1,675 to £2,500. Motor Import Ltd later moved to the Naas Road.

Nowadays, the estate is disused, awaiting re-development. The adjoining house is also called Glenville, built in the early 1930's for Dr John Ralph. It is two storey over semi-basement, with a hint of a nautical theme in its appearance.

158

Glenville Estate is centre rear, with white roof. Merville in UCD on lower right. (PB)

Motor Import Ltd in Glenville Estate, 1968: BMW 2000.

Foster Motors

This started off as Eames garage in the early 1960's, presumably the same family who owned the garage where Esso is now located in Greygates. In the late 1960's it was called Eames and Wynne, and this continued until the mid

1990's, when Foster Motors was established, specialising in Volkswagen and Audi cars. These days, the showroom is in Stillorgan Industrial Park.

Crèches and Pre-Schools

In the old days, the father was the "bread winner", and the mother looked after the home, usually including six or more children, which in itself was more than a full time job. In addition, once a woman got married, she had to resign from her job, as required by Civil Service rules, and this practice was adopted in most big companies, including banks etc., although the ban was lifted a few decades ago. Nowadays, family sizes have reduced to a national average of two and a quarter children, with the result that more women opt to remain in their chosen career. Furthermore, with the huge increases in house prices over the past decade, many families need both parents to work, in order to pay for a large mortgage. Crèches sprang up like mushrooms, to mind babies while the parents were at work. Most of the crèches were simply a spare room in someone's house, filled with toys, so that a parent could hand in a child early in the morning, and collect the child that evening. Once a toddler reached four years of age, they started in National School, so the crèche would only receive the child after school hours. Alongside this development, pre-schools emerged, providing a little tuition in reading etc for children aged 2 to 4. The end result is that many modern children rarely see their parents during the week, and their very important formative years are influenced by strangers. Like the rest of the country, Mount Merrion has its share of crèches and pre-schools, some very small, others occupying a whole building.

Slievemore Medical Centre

In recent years, a welcome addition to the locality has been this lovely facility, directly opposite the front of Oatlands College on the Old Dublin Road. The original detached house has been extensively remodelled and extended, and now contains the rooms of various family doctors, a dentist, a pharmacy, and some specialists, but no optician. Obviously there is still a variety of doctors and dentists operating from houses scattered around the suburb.

Chapter 20

KIELYS - STELLA

David Ronald Whitren is the businessman who built Stella House in the late 1950's. He had planned to build it across the road on the site of the present children's playground, but it was deemed to be too near the new Catholic Church. David, an electronics engineer, was born in Canada in 1925, and came to Ireland in 1952. His original building comprised 12 flatlets, a dance hall, and two businesses, Irish Television Maintenance Ltd, and Electricraft Ltd.

1989 view of former Stella, before the addition of various pitched roofs. (MA)

2009 view

161

In the 1960's, and to a lesser extent in the 1970's, the Stella Ballroom attracted up-and-coming new bands, such as Them from Belfast, which included Van Morrison in the line-up. David also managed his own band called The Stellas, a variation of the showband era, featuring such instruments as guitar, rhythm guitar, bass guitar, keyboard, drums, tenor saxophone, baritone saxophone, etc. In those days, there was no alcohol available in ballrooms, and this trend continued for some decades.

Then the venue became a public house called The Sportmans Inn, from 1980 – 1986, still operated by David Whitren, and was very popular for music gigs, featuring such Irish bands as Full Circle.

From 1986 – 1993, the pub was called Mount Merrion House, and owned by Toby Restaurants, a subsidiary of Bass, a large British brewery. Toby completely modernized the premises, and greatly improved the outside "boxy" appearance, by putting red tiled pitched roofs on top of the various flat roofs. The different areas had familiar titles, such as, the Rise Lounge, the Cedar Room (a small function room), the Summit suite (a function room on the first floor) and the Fitzwilliam Restaurant on the lower ground floor. There was outside parking for 120 cars.

"Cheers"

By the mid 1990's, the pub had again changed hands, this time to Kielys of Donnybrook, who naturally enough renamed it Kielys. They created a separate bar, fitted out exactly as an old-time bar, with very little in the way of creature comforts. Adult dances were held at weekends in the first floor function room (called Cheers). These dances were organized by popular DJ Mike Fallon for about 18years, but ceased two years ago due to competition from hotels holding Afternoon Tea dances. The basement restaurant seems to change hands

162

periodically, from Peking cuisine to Thai, to Chinese, etc. Recently music gigs have returned to the main lounge, and Full Circle are back again to entertain the crowds. There is now a small music museum in the front of the lounge.

♣

Just to confuse matters, the adjoining premises was a large 1,000 seater cinema called the Stella, built in 1955 by the O'Grady family, who also owned the Stella cinema in Rathmines. The first film was Ring of Fear (about a circus), starring Clyde Beatty and Mickey Spillane, and admission prices were 1/6 (one shilling and six pence) for the stalls, and 2/6 for the balcony. The following week, Valley of the Eagles, was shown, supported by Cave of Outlaws. In the mid 1960's, a typical show might be I'm all Right Jack, supported by Two Way Stretch, both starring Peter Sellers. In the mid 1970's, a good evening out could comprise Deliverance, supported by Dirty Harry, the latter starring Clint Eastwood. The 1970's saw the demise of many suburban cinemas, or subdivision into multiplex screens, largely because the price of television sets dropped, and most houses could now afford to buy a colour TV set. The Stella closed in October 1976, with a final showing of Earthquake, starring Charlton Heston, Ava Gardner and George Kennedy. The building was then acquired by Flanagan's of Buncrana, an upmarket household furniture shop, which was founded in Donegal in 1946. They did not alter the building, and you can still see the ornate 1950's plasterwork, some terrazzo flooring, and even the letters SC on the floor in the porch. The present display windows were originally two little shops, unconnected with the cinema - some people might remember Speight School of Motoring in the left hand shop.

Former Stella Cinema, now Flanagans Furniture.

163

Chapter 21

Miscellaneous

Trimleston Stream

Clair Sweeney in his wonderful book, The Rivers of Dublin, describes this little stream, much of it now culverted (piped underground). It starts in Mount Merrion, just south of St Therese Church, and flows downhill towards the back gardens between St Thomas Road and Fosters Avenue, then to the Stillorgan Road, which it crosses, running to the north of St Helens Hotel (Radisson), and east towards the Merrion Road, and on into the sea. Some locals still remember an open stream in the 1940/50's in the St Thomas Road area, and at least two house names are reminders of this, Burnside (burn is Scottish for stream), and Gaybrook, just beside the bottom of North Avenue. In fact, the 1928 development plan for the demesne envisaged a pleasure garden and boating lake between Fosters Ave and St Thomas Road, but part of this area became the present Glenville Industrial Estate. A tributary of the stream is still visible in the grounds of UCD, parallel to Fosters Avenue.

Priory Stream

Little is known about this stream, although it appears to have been associated with Darleys Brewery in Brewery Road, Stillorgan. Nowadays, it runs through an open ditch between Priory Avenue and Linden Apartments, crossing Priory Ave alongside No 3, and runs off towards Grove Ave and down to Blackrock.

Stillorgan Road

Up until the 1970's, tree-lined Stillorgan Road was narrow and winding, with little traffic. However, various events in the 1960's heralded increased traffic, such as the opening of UCD in Belfield, Montrose hotel opposite, RTE in Donnybrook, Stilllorgan Shopping Centre, and Bowling Alley opposite. Hence, the Belfield fly-over was built in 1974, and the road widened between Nutley Lane and Booterstown Ave. The Stillorgan By-pass was officially opened in 1979, and the Booterstown Ave to Trees Road section was widened in the early 1980's. The end result was the N11, a National Road, which isolated the eastern part of Mount Merrion parish. Many front gardens in Greygates and elsewhere were reduced in size, and Mount Merrion Gardens shops were demolished. Part of St Helen's estate was cut off, resulting in an abandoned and overgrown triangular shaped wooded park, opposite houses 1-6, Greygates, including the old granite boundary wall. The car ended the glory-days of Mount Merrion, since people could travel outside the parish to schools, shops, entertainment etc.

Bomb Shelters

Many older residents fondly remember the Second World War period (The Emergency in neutral Ireland), since all sorts of Local Defence Forces and Action Groups were mustered, in case Ireland was invaded by Britain or Germany. These groups were like Boy Scouts for adults, and brought great comraderie to the community. Bomb Shelters are a reminder of this era, some of which survive in the odd back garden. 28 Greygates still has its above-ground 3metre high conical shelter, made of mass concrete, about 2 metres diameter at the base, tapering to about 450mm and a vent opening at the top. There are two low door openings, but no windows. In effect, it looks like a wig-wam.

Allotments

Allotments are not readily associated with affluent Mount Merrion and its spacious back gardens. However, there are public allotments to the west of Knockrabo, opposite Mount Anville schools, extending to about 9 acres. Plots are 15 foot by 40 foot, and 25 foot by 50 foot, with minimal or no fencing, and rented by the County Council for €32 per annum (€6.35 to O.A.P. and unemployed). There is currently a waiting list. The plots are used for growing all kinds of vegetables, and some flowers, and little makeshift huts have sprung up here and there. The Council acquired the land in 1977 for a new road, but for the present, it remains a beautiful peaceful oasis of rural living.

ESB Transformer Station

Almost hidden away beside Sycamore Lodge lies a little gem of architecture, very similar in appearance to many rural cinemas. This single storey concrete building has a lovely Art Deco 1930's façade, and runs back to form a long narrow building. The painted render on the façade is given the classical treatment with pilasters and vertical fluting, and has two front entrances. The side elevations also have fluted features, and even the piers for the wrought iron gates are curved and fluted. The station reduces the voltage from 38 kilovolts to 10 kV, and is an important hub for Mount Merrion, Kilmacud, Goatstown, Booterstown and Blackrock.

Art Deco ESB Transformer Station

Telephone Exchange

Not half as attractive is the 1960's single storey exchange at the corner of Priory Drive and the N11, with its rear two storey 1970's extension. The addition of a tall steel lattice mobile phone mast, does nothing to enhance the ensemble.

Letterboxes

These days, e-mailing by internet, and texting on mobile phones, have replaced a lot of letter post, but An Post is still a thriving business, and relies on public letterboxes to collect the mail, most dating from the Victorian era. Before Irelands independence in 1922, all post boxes were painted red (as they still are in Northern Ireland and Britain), and the new Government simply overpainted them green. Most have royal insignia or logos, depending on the reigning monarch when the iron box was cast. There are still two basic types of post box – the free-standing circular pillar box, and the inbuilt wall box. Mount Merion has some interesting boxes, some of which were supplied from old stock, or removed from another location in Ireland.

The pillar box outside Super Valu on The Rise, has the interwoven logo VR, referring to Regina Victoria, who reigned from 1837 to 1901. It was made by Andrew Handyside of Derby (England), in the period 1887-93. A similar one in Sycamore Road dates from 1893-1901.

The pillar box outside McGuires sweet shop in Deerpark Road was made by Carron Co of Scotland, probably in the 1950's, and has the logo P&T - Dept. of Posts and Telegraphs. The latter body split in 1984 into An Post and Telecom Eireann (now Eircom plc). There is a similar box at the top of Trees Road Upper. The box in Cherrygarth has 1960's features, and is also by Carron Co, Stirlingshire.

One of the most historic wall boxes is on Fosters Ave, beside the former Foster Motors. This displays the Saorstat Eireann logo, with the letters S and E, together with a harp. After Independence in 1922, the 26 counties were called Saorstat Eireann, or Irish Free State. The S.E. logo was used on letterboxes from 1922-25, after which P&T was used. The S.E. logo was applied to the doors of older boxes. The box on Fosters Ave was made by W. T. Allen & Co of London, probably in the 1880's, and it is probable that the letters V and R, and crown, were removed from the space above the letter flap. Just up the road on Mt Anville Rd, opposite the entrance to Mount Anville Park, is a similar wall box, with Queen Victoria symbols, from the period 1887-1904. Another disused box at the bottom of Fosters Ave, opposite St Thomas Church, has had its symbols ground off.

On Grove Ave, off Mount Merrion Ave, there is a wall box, with the letters G and R, and a crown, above the letter flap, dating from the reign of George V (1911-36).

On the old Stillorgan Road, between Oatlands and Trees Road, is a large wall box, with P & T logo, made by Jessop Davis of Enniscorthy (Wexford), a noteworthy Quaker milling family. Their St Johns Foundry operated for most of the first half of the 20th century, and the Oatlands box may date from the 1950's.

All of the foregoing items of "street furniture" constitute very good examples of our industrial heritage, and should be used for as long as possible, and then preserved in the National Museum.

Former Foster Motors.
Historic Saorstat Eireann letterbox on wall under auctioneers board.

Famous People

People with Mount Merrion connections include TV newsreader, Don Cockburn, TV broadcaster, Vere Wynne Jones, singer, Alma Carroll, newspaper magnate and Heinz executive, Tony O'Reilly, and many more. General Eoin O'Duffy lived in 44 Greygates, and church builder, John du Moulin, lived in 45 Greygates, having founded his building company in 1937.

Builder and developer, **Liam Carroll**, originally from Co Louth, still lives in Mount Merrion. In the mid 1980's, he spearheaded the explosion in apartment living in modern Ireland, by building reasonably priced medium-rise blocks in run-down parts of Dublin, thereby bringing life back into the capital, and halting the erosion of the green belt around Dublin. Up until then, large sprawling estates of mediocre three-bedroom semi-detached houses were the norm on greenfield sites, while the inner city areas became derelict. Liam was one of the biggest apartment block developers in Dublin, although he was also active in many commercial developments, all under the umbrella of the Zoe Group.

The **Smurfit** family, who originally hailed from England, have a long association with the area, firstly their home in 66 Trees Road, and then in Tyne Villa, opposite Oatlands College on the old Stillorgan Road. The latter house was built as a luxury bungalow in the early 1960's, with access off a neighbour's driveway, but was recently remodelled and greatly enlarged, and provided with its own entrance, and is still occupied by a family member. Possibly the most famous Smurfit, after Jefferson, is his son, Michael, who now heads a world-wide paper packaging empire.

Kevin Hilton, who lived on The Rise during the 1950/60's, was famous throughout Dublin for his ability to organise and compere, and sometimes participate in, cabarets, which were live variety concerts, with singers, dancers, comedians, magicians etc.

Comedian, **Dermot Morgan**, was born and raised in Wilson Road, and he is best remembered for the hilarious ITV television series Father Ted, although he was also involved in RTE programmes, including Scrap Saturday. Sadly, he died in 1998, aged only forty six. The city council honoured him by erecting a bronze "high chair" in Merrion Square park, recognising that he was a big man in many ways.

Garda **Anthony Tighe** from Ranelagh, and Garda **Michael Padden** from Belmullet in Mayo, both based in Donnybrook Station, lost their lives in 2002, at a checkpoint where The Rise meets the Stillorgan Road, while trying to stop a high-speed stolen car. A granite memorial stone has been erected by the Garda Siochana, in the shadow of a pair of nearby mature chestnut trees.

President **Eamon de Valera** died in the Linden Nursing Home, in nearby Grove Avenue, in 1975, and the photo below shows the funeral cortege, with gun-carriage, passing the South County Hotel (now the Stillorgan Park Hotel). Notice Texaco Garage and shops behind, and Mount Merrion House on left.

President Eamon de Valera's funeral cortege/gun-carriage passing Greygates in 1975.

Other Books by the same Author

Times, Chimes & Charms of Dublin (2nd Edition 2010)

Harolds Cross (3rd Edition, reprinted 2009)

Haslam's Gold, 2009

Thanks God, You're a Real Pal

Great Landmarks in Time

9189875R0

Made in the USA
Lexington, KY
05 April 2011